How to Find the Love of your Life

12 Principles from the Greatest Family Marriage Dynasty

NG Enelamah

Eight Romans

Copyright © NG Enelamah 2022

NG Enelamah has asserted her right to be identified as the author of this work following the Copyright, Designs and Patents Act 1988.

No part of this publication may be reproduced or transmitted in any form or by any means, mechanical or electronic, including photocopying or recording, or by any information and retrieval system, without permission in writing from the author or publisher (except for quotes of brief passages with author's name and source acknowledged).

All scripture references and sources in italics throughout the text are found in the endnotes.

First published in the United States by Eight Romans Educational Resources in 2022.

ISBN: 9798425289049

Inspiration | Self-help | Faith

To papa, Chief Ukachi Ikemba

Who wrote me in Dec 1997: "...*Johnny, late Rev. Enelamah's son came to visit us and asked of you? Now, I'm not suggesting that anybody should marry anybody, but he seems quite like a fine Christian of the kind you profess....*"

Table of Contents

Preface		7
Prologue		11
Part I	**Partnership with the Divine**	**17**
1	Is there not a cause?	18
2	The principle of Divine activity	23
3	The principle of prayer	35
4	The principle of the assignment	44
5	The principle of timing	58
Part II	**Marriage Is a Family Affair**	**71**
6	The principle of equal yokes	72
7	The principle of parental honor	88
8	The principle of gifts	102
9	The principle of service	117
Part III	**To be, before you do and have**	**128**
10	The principle of dedication	129
11	The principle of purity	136
12	The principle of focus	145
13	The principle of attraction	159
14	The will of God	173
Endnotes		179
Acknowledgements		182

Preface

I started writing the draft for this book a couple of years ago when my dearest husband and pastor asked me to teach singles about how to make the right choice in marriage. We had started a church and as a young couple, we found ourselves having to conduct weddings — ranging from joining young lovers to prospective blended families. It was daunting. We counseled and troubleshot marriages and walked families through challenging times. One of the things that struck me was how some people who seemed to me to have no business together were stuck in a marriage. Life circumstances, wrong motives and, sheer lack of perspective on the power of the marriage choice had resulted in regretful relationships. For some, life's challenges threatened relationships that were obviously made in heaven. The issues were often heartbreaking for the couples and us as we tried to work with them and, not always successfully. Relationship problems are some of the most painful and have been shown to affect mental and physical health and overall progress in life.

My husband and I have trained and continue to provide instruction to singles and engaged and married couples, both one-on-one and through structured seminars. As members of the marriage counseling team in our church, we have identified and continue to observe the challenges faced by couples and how they could have been prevented. It is clear to me that the books I had read as I prepared to get married, as well as the single and married sessions I attended, and the detailed premarital counseling sessions we had have served my marriage well. More so, my life experiences, the benefit of witnessing my parents' over 50 years of marriage, and indeed God's word – all helped me to understand relationships, including how to navigate mine. I assure you our marriage is by no means perfect. We have had and still have tough times. We do not agree on many issues, but I can say that we are a positive and optimistic work in progress. We are friends, committed to our love for each other, continuous improvement, and to making the best of our marriage.

Marriage is an important aspect of life (for those called to marry), and the second most important destiny decision we make, after choosing the direction of our faith or spiritual alignment. My husband and I strongly believe that couples can avoid unnecessary pain and heartbreak if they learn the ropes of a loving and working relationship. As with most things in life, it is better to prepare ahead of time, rather than having to learn while in a relationship. Unmarried men and women will be in a better position to succeed in marriage prepared, before they meet 'the one,' rather than during or after the fact, especially since it is more difficult to objectively address issues if they have become emotionally involved.

One of the books on marriage that I enjoyed reading after I got married was by a well-known author, and expert on marriage, Gary Chapman. He began with an introduction from Genesis 24: Abraham's search for a wife for his son Isaac. He highlighted some points that helped Abraham succeed on that mission. I recognized that these had worked for me, albeit unknown to me at that time, and for several other couples who shared their experiences with us. As I studied the Genesis 24 chapter, I found more principles in the story, and I would teach these in my classes. Whenever I share these lessons with others, I am always grateful for the impact on their lives. As we discuss issues in marriages, which include the decision and the process of committing to the relationship, these principles from Genesis 24 so often become obvious. This book is about those principles from Genesis 24.

Abraham, patriarch to the world's most influential faiths—Judaism, Islam, and Christianity—has both a physical and spiritual lineage that has endured for many generations. We are still reading and learning from the story of Abraham's great family and marriage dynasty today, and it all began when he entered a covenant with God. The relationship guided Abraham's decisions, including choosing a wife for his son who would continue the family's legacy.

Neil Warren Clark in his book, *Finding the Love of your Life* said, "the choice of whom to marry is more important than anything else you will ever do to make your marriage work." I define "anything else" to include marriage counseling, great sex, friends, gifts, wealth, and all the antics that could add value to the marriage. They are not nearly as important as 'the who.' Each person must work hard on themselves to be the right 'who' in the relationship. When you are the right who, it becomes easier to find and choose the one. The choice of whom Abraham's promised and long-awaited son would marry was a huge burden for him. He could not afford the family to make a mistake.

This book highlights the principles or unchanging pillars of success in becoming and choosing 'the who' in the destiny-defining relationship called marriage. People have violated many of these principles over time and the mercy of God finds them. Yet, these principles, if leveraged, have the power to distinguish and immensely redefine for good, your relationship, marriage, and indeed, your whole life.

The book is divided into three parts. In the prologue, we read the Genesis 24 story of Abraham's quest for a wife for his son and how he worked with his chief servant, whom we will assume is Eliezer to achieve this goal. This story will be our case study. We will follow how Isaac successfully found his wife and became the essential progenitor of the Judeo-Christian dynasty and family lineage. The principles identified in this book are supported by action steps (outlined in a workbook that follows) to enable you to apply them to obtain momentous results just like Abraham's family did. The sequel to this book, *This relationship called marriage*, explores the purpose and benefits of the marriage relationship.

My husband and I are passionate about marriages and thriving families and want to see more loving, fruitful, and lasting relationships. We and so many couples with whom we have worked and interacted have experienced the benefits of the principles enumerated in this book. Many couples that enjoy their marriage can attest that the principles in this book if applied, will bring great results. Marriage is meant to be the most beautiful and most intimate relationship of human beings on earth. Your marriage will so affect your life that it is never an area that you should enter casually or compromise. Ed Young said, *'Life is too short to spend hooked to the wrong partner.'* Marriage is a union fashioned in heaven to be enjoyed on earth. God is a great planner and the ultimate Matchmaker. Whatever God does is impressive and beautiful, and your marriage will not be an exception. If your life's path includes marriage, then this book is for you. Follow these principles in your choice and watch yourself step into the marriage of destiny prepared for you.

Feel free to start from any chapter to read. As you apply the principles illustrated in this book, my prayer is that God will prepare, equip, and lead you to the one He has prepared you for, and vice versa. I pray this book is a blessing to you!

NG Enelamah

Prologue[1]

Abraham was now an old man. God had blessed Abraham in every way.

Abraham spoke to the senior servant in his household, the one in charge of everything he had, "Put your hand under my thigh and swear by God—God of Heaven, God of Earth—that you will not get a wife for my son from among the young women of the Canaanites here, but will go to the land of my birth and get a wife for my son Isaac."

The servant answered, "But what if the woman refuses to leave home and come with me? Do I then take your son back to your home country?"

Abraham said, "Oh no. Never. By no means are you to take my son back there. God, the God of Heaven, took me from the home of my father and from the country of my birth and spoke to me in solemn promise, 'I'm giving this land to your descendants.' This God will send his angel ahead of you to get a wife for my son. And if the woman won't come, you are free from this oath you've sworn to me. But under no circumstances are you to take my son back there."

So the servant put his hand under the thigh of his master Abraham and gave his solemn oath.

The servant took ten of his master's camels and, loaded with gifts from his master, traveled to Aram Naharaim and the city of Nahor. Outside the city, he made the camels kneel at a well. It was evening, the time when the women came to draw water. He prayed, "O GOD, God of my master Abraham, make things go smoothly this day; treat my master Abraham well! As I stand here by the spring while the young women of the town come out to get water, let the girl to whom I say, 'Lower your jug and give me a drink,' and who answers, 'Drink, and let me also water your camels'—let her be the woman you have picked out for your servant Isaac. Then I'll know that you're working graciously behind the scenes for my master."

It so happened that the words were barely out of his mouth when Rebekah, the daughter of Bethuel whose mother was Milcah the wife of Nahor, Abraham's brother, came out with a water jug on her shoulder. The girl was stunningly beautiful, a pure virgin. She went down to the spring, filled her jug, and came back up. The servant ran to meet her and said, "Please, can I have a sip of water from your jug?"

She said, "Certainly, drink!" And she held the jug so that he could drink. When he had satisfied his thirst she said, "I'll get water for your camels, too, until they've drunk their fill." She promptly emptied her jug into the trough and ran back to the well to fill it, and she kept at it until she had watered all the camels.

The man watched, silent. Was this GOD's answer? Had GOD made his trip a success or not?

When the camels had finished drinking, the man brought out gifts, a gold nose ring weighing a little over a quarter of an ounce and two arm bracelets weighing about four ounces and gave them to her. He asked her, "Tell me about your family? Whose daughter are you? Is there room in your father's house for us to stay the night?"

She said, "I'm the daughter of Bethuel the son of Milcah and Nahor. And there's plenty of room in our house for you to stay—and lots of straw and feed besides."

At this the man bowed in worship before God and prayed, "Blessed be God, God of my master Abraham: How generous and true you've been to my master; you've held nothing back. You led me right to the door of my master's brother!"

And the girl was off and running, telling everyone in her mother's house what had happened.

Rebekah had a brother named Laban. Laban ran outside to the man at the spring. He had seen the nose ring and the bracelets on his sister and had heard her say, "The man said this and this and this to me." So he went to the man and there he was, still standing with his camels at the spring. Laban welcomed him: "Come on in, blessed of God! Why are you standing out here? I've got the house ready for you; and there's also a place for your camels."

So, the man went into the house. The camels were unloaded and given straw and feed. Water was brought to bathe the feet of the man and the men with him. Then Laban brought out food. But the man said, "I won't eat until I tell my story."

Laban said, "Go ahead; tell us."

The servant said, "I'm the servant of Abraham. God has blessed my master—he's a great man; God has given him sheep and cattle, silver and gold, servants and maidservants, camels and donkeys. And then to top it off, Sarah, my master's wife, gave him a son in her old age and he has passed

Principles from the Greatest Family Marriage Dynasty

everything on to his son. My master made me promise, 'Don't get a wife for my son from the daughters of the Canaanites in whose land I live. No, go to my father's home, back to my family, and get a wife for my son there.' I said to my master, 'But what if the woman won't come with me?' He said, 'GOD before whom I've walked faithfully will send his angel with you and he'll make things work out so that you'll bring back a wife for my son from my family, from the house of my father. Then you'll be free from the oath. If you go to my family and they won't give her to you, you will also be free from the oath.'

"Well, when I came this very day to the spring, I prayed, 'GOD, God of my master Abraham, make things turn out well in this task I've been given. I'm standing at this well. When a young woman comes here to draw water and I say to her, Please, give me a sip of water from your jug, and she says, Not only will I give you a drink, I'll also water your camels—let that woman be the wife GOD has picked out for my master's son.'

"I had barely finished offering this prayer, when Rebekah arrived, her jug on her shoulder. She went to the spring and drew water and I said, 'Please, can I have a drink?' She didn't hesitate. She held out her jug and said, 'Drink; and when you're finished, I'll also water your camels.' I drank, and she watered the camels. I asked her, 'Whose daughter are you?' She said, 'The daughter of Bethuel whose parents were Nahor and Milcah.' I gave her a ring for her nose, bracelets for her arms, and bowed in worship to GOD. I praised GOD, the God of my master Abraham who had led me straight to the door of my master's family to get a wife for his son.

"Now, tell me what you are going to do. If you plan to respond with a generous yes, tell me. But if not, tell me plainly so I can figure out what to do next."

Laban and Bethuel answered, "This is undeniably from God. We have no say in the matter, either yes or no. Rebekah is yours: Take her and go; let her be the wife of your master's son, as God has made plain."

When Abraham's servant heard their decision, he bowed in worship before God. Then he brought out gifts of silver, gold, and clothing and gave them to Rebekah. He also gave expensive gifts to her brother and mother. He and his men had supper and spent the night. But first thing in the morning they were up. He said, "Send me back to my master."

Her brother and mother said, "Let the girl stay a while, say another ten days, and then go."

He said, "Oh, don't make me wait! God has worked everything out so well—send me off to my master."

They said, "We'll call the girl; we'll ask her."

They called Rebekah and asked her, "Do you want to go with this man?"

She said, "I'm ready to go."

So, they sent them off, their sister Rebekah with her nurse, and Abraham's servant with his men. And they blessed Rebekah saying,

   You're our sister—live bountifully! And your children, triumphantly!

Rebekah and her young maids mounted the camels and followed the man. The servant took Rebekah and set off for home.

Isaac was living in the Negev. He had just come back from a visit to Beer Lahai Roi. In the evening he went out into the field; while meditating he

Principles from the Greatest Family Marriage Dynasty

looked up and saw camels coming. When Rebekah looked up and saw Isaac, she got down from her camel and asked the servant, "Who is that man out in the field coming toward us?"

"That is my master."

She took her veil and covered herself.

After the servant told Isaac the whole story of the trip, Isaac took Rebekah into the tent of his mother Sarah. He married Rebekah and she became his wife and he loved her. So, Isaac found comfort after his mother's death.

* * *

Part I
Partnership with the Divine

Take care to live in me and let me live in you. For a branch can't produce fruit when severed from the vine. Nor can you be fruitful apart from me. "Yes, I am the Vine; you are the branches. Whoever lives in me and I in him shall produce... For apart from me you can't do a thing.[2]

Chapter 1
Is there not a cause?

And David said, what have I now done? Is there not a cause?[3]

For many years before I got married, I attended relationships seminars. During some of those sessions, we were asked to write the qualities we wanted in a spouse. Being no stranger to fantasy and love stories, I wrote avidly. I knew what I wanted and kept my elaborate list close to heart, and in my precious Bible. For a long while, I would often read and pray over it. I wrote a lot about the man I would spend the rest of my life loving. Looking back, keeping that list close by felt great and brought great hope toward my goal and the desire for a great marriage. Over time and after different life experiences, I had to let go of my idealistic list and yield to whatever plan God would have for me. I realized that I had no control over who my spouse would be, when the marriage would be, nor of how our lives would play out. In life, you live, work, play, and sleep – but in the hours of sleep, you have absolutely no control or knowledge of anything till you wake up. As much as contemporary life wants to make us believe that we have control over our lives, there are so many things that will happen the very next day that we are not able to predict. When the answer to my prayers seemed delayed, I began to feel desperate. It was no longer about my list of what I wanted in a spouse, it was more like God, please, don't leave me hanging? Several years later, God graciously connected me to my husband, and I could not have orchestrated a better match.

However, during the times that I thought, wrote, and prayed about the qualities that I wanted in a spouse, I neither considered nor bothered about the purpose of marriage. I was more interested in just being happy and married. I fantasized about who my spouse would be - tall, dark, handsome, and rich? I thought of what we would look like as a couple, our children, the exciting life we would share, and all the places we would go. I imagined that my mum would be happy and satisfied that the last of her five girls had settled into her own home (remember *Pride and Prejudice*). I loved God and wanted to please Him in all I do, but I never considered God's perspective on marriage or that He might have specific expectations for my marriage.

The desire to get married is different for everyone. For instance, for some women, at a certain age or level of education, there is often an innate desire or societal pressure to get married and start a family. Men are not left out, though not as visibly vexed as women. When most men have a sense of a career path, coupled with a decent income, they feel they are ready to commit or are similarly pressured by family or peers to do so. Some others enjoy their freedom to live single, footloose, and fancy-free for much longer and shy away from any situation that tries to tie them down.

For those that wish for marriage, as they approach that season of life, they are often unconsciously searching for their mate; the person whom they think would complete their lives and fulfill the deepest longings of their hearts. It is inbuilt in nearly every creature. Now and then, and mostly when single and searching, you enter a room and find yourself surveying the occupants. And when someone attracts your attention, you wonder if they are 'the one' while comparing them with your mental image of a spouse. The gracious thing is that somewhere along the journey of life, that partner of your mental image exists. And the best part is that God is eager to connect you to the one. You only need to believe that it is possible.

All Things are Possible

I have met many people who have struggled with so much hurt, disappointment, and betrayals that they doubt a great marriage is ever possible. The truth is you can have a marriage beyond your dreams, and that is God's original plan. God's promises are unchanging. Irrespective of what you have been through in life, all things are possible if you believe: you can find your spouse made just for you and enjoy the marriage of your dreams. Sometimes life throws you a curveball, and you meet challenging situations from which only a Divine power could have rescued you. I have been there too many times; God always comes through. God can do all things if you can trust and walk with Him. He is Almighty God.

Abraham and Sarah received the promise of a son even though they were old and had passed the fruitful years of conception. They even had to wait more years after God made the promise for it to be fulfilled. God said to Abraham, *"Is anything too hard for the LORD? I will come back to you next year at this time, and Sarah will have a son."*[4] In another instance, God spoke to Jeremiah: *"I am the Lord, the God of all the peoples of the world. Is anything too hard for me?"*[5] God specializes in what is impossible to man. Jesus also said, *"Humanly speaking, it is impossible. But with God everything is possible."* [6]

Man is progressively unraveling the entirety of what God created for him to enjoy on earth. God has given man so much intelligence to discover and experience life. Solomon said, *"It is the glory of God to conceal matters and (the glory of) man to search them out."* [7] Would life not be boring, monotonous, and overwhelming if you knew everything about your life and how it would unfold – where you would live, people you would meet, whom you would marry, and when or how you would die? That is often our preference – and we go to so many lengths to seek predictions, control our life's outcomes, and secure the future.

Although the institution of marriage is ancient, people still want to get married. No matter how postmodern we become, the marriage relationship is still desired and has not become outdated. You would think that by now, with all the science and innovation, we should understand how marriage works and excel through all its intricacies.

Yet, our vast knowledge of science and the understanding of human psychology and relationship dynamics are grossly inadequate to invent great marriages. People are still unable to predict that a well-planned and executed wedding will be a great marriage. We are unable to use all our wealth and comforts to ensure a happy union. We need God, the originator of life, and Who instituted marriage to understand the union. The Apostle Paul described marriage as a mystery: … *"A man leaves his father and mother and is joined to his wife, and the two are united into one. This is a great mystery…"* [8]

Marriage is Serious Business

The decision to get married should not be careless and should not be taken lightly. It is better to be single than to get married without a complete understanding of the consequences of your choice. Your marriage will either make or break you. While there will always be challenges in life and relationships – no one is perfect, you can be guaranteed a beautiful marriage if you understand the principles for a successful marriage and are both willing to apply God's wisdom.

When God made Adam, he took a rib from Adam to create Eve. Why did God do that? He did not create Eve the same way He had created Adam from the earth. God wanted Eve to come from Adam. She would be from his body, a part of him. I have heard and read amazing stories from different continents of how couples met or came together, the connection they felt, and how they knew they had found their soulmate. Life happens in patterns. The first marriage on earth between Adam and Eve says a rib was taken from a man to form his wife. There is someone for you. People ask, is there only one person for each one? I say you cannot put God in a box -circumstances of a life changes - death, challenges, and exceptions to this pattern will occur. Much of life is a bell curve.

Jesus was asked why the law of Moses allowed divorce in some instances. *Some Pharisees came to him to test him. They asked, "Is it proper for a man to divorce his wife for any and every reason?" "Haven't you read," he replied, "that at the beginning the Creator 'made them male and female,' and said, 'For this reason, a man will leave his father and mother and be united to his wife, and the two will become one flesh? So, they are no longer two but one flesh. Therefore, what God has joined together, let no one separate." "Why then," they asked, "did Moses command that a man give his wife a certificate of divorce and send her away?"*

Jesus replied, "Moses permitted you to divorce your wives because your hearts were hard. But it was not this way from the beginning.[9] Jesus's reply implied that it is best to focus on God's original plan when considering marriage. And that is where we take our viewpoint from, not the exceptions. How was it from the beginning? That is the focus of this book.

Chapter 2
The principle of Divine activity

'Then the Lord God said, "It is not good for the man to be alone. I will make a helper who is just right for him."

From the prologue, we see the story of the patriarch, Abraham, and how he was intentional in the quest for a wife for his son Isaac. Before Abraham sent his assistant on this assignment, he had had some unique experiences with God. Abraham had received instructions asking him to offer Isaac his only son as a sacrifice. Abraham went ahead with the plan – with a willing accomplice, Isaac. Isaac could have easily outrun his old papa and prevented him from trying to prepare him, Isaac, as the sacrifice. He could have easily escaped. Instead of running away, he went along with Abraham's plan, trusting that Abraham's decision was informed and for the best. Abraham would later use a lamb in a nearby thicket for the sacrifice in place of Isaac.

Through this test and other experiences, Abraham and Isaac established a relationship with God and proved to be men who wanted to live lives that pleased God. From this one child, Isaac, the nation of Israel would evolve and shape a significant part of human history. Abraham's priority in life was to see that God's promises and instructions to him were accomplished. God was the center stage of the life of Abraham and his family. Isaac, the spouse-seeking young man, had grown to see that there was a God at work in their lives. Therefore, when it was time to get married, Isaac was with his father in their commitment to seeing that God had a say in the matter.

The choice of a spouse for Isaac was essential to the fulfilling of the promise from God. More so, like any good father, Abraham was interested and actively involved in Isaac's future. He figured that if God would be so specific about Sarah being the heir's mother and not the other woman who had borne a child for him, Hagar, then He certainly had a plan for the woman the heir, Isaac, would marry.

It was no surprise then that Abraham was involved in this search for a wife for his son, which in many cases will be different from how families operate today. Today, you hear the prompts to exercise your agency, follow your heart, your choice, and go for it. Many people today will not let anyone, let alone their dad, be involved in choosing a spouse for them. However, some people have told me though, that they like the safety of some form of structured 'arrangement' or being introduced to a reliable prospective partner but are often ashamed to admit it because of popular culture.

Nonetheless, Abraham's personal and covenant relationship with the Divine Being made a difference in the wife-search. He knew that if God had led him to succeed in business, family, and social life, he could trust Him for a wife for his son, Isaac. Abraham was working from the principle of divine activity. The principle of divine activity is about the sovereignty of God over life. It is about acknowledging and partnering with God, the Divine One over the workings of your life.

The principle of divine activity states that there is a Sovereign God, the Most-High God, the Maker of the heavens and the earth, the Creator of man, the Original Matchmaker - Who rules in the affairs of men, working behind the scenes, and orchestrating the details of your life, including marriage. Divine activity is not about fathers finding wives for their sons but about the heavenly Father, full of wisdom, who knows what is best for you and desires to lead you, if you accept, to His plan for your life.

The first match

God created the heavens and the earth. He saw the goodness in all that He had created. He watched with pleasure as the man named the other creatures and went about his assignment of managing the garden of Eden, and its affairs. *'Then the Lord God said, "It is not good for the man to be alone. I will make a helper who is just right for him." So, the Lord God formed from the ground all the wild animals and all the birds of the sky. He brought them to the man to see what he would call them, and the man chose a name for each one. He gave names to all the livestock, all the birds of the sky, and all the wild animals. But still, there was no helper just right for him. So, the Lord God caused the man to fall into a deep sleep. While the man slept, the Lord God took out one of the man's ribs and closed up the opening. Then the Lord God made a woman from the rib, and he brought her to the man.*[10]

Working behind the scenes

God saw Adam's situation – alone and without support, and while Adam slept, God took a rib from him to form the woman and brought her to the man to become his wife. It was God's idea and initiative, God's plan, God's orchestration, and God's action that set the marriage machinery in motion. God instituted marriage and designed the man and the woman to be together. This

> *The principle of divine activity states that there is a Sovereign God who rules in the affairs of men, orchestrating the details of life - including marriage, which is His original idea.*

is the principle of divine activity. Before you even begin to think that you need a relationship or that you would like to get married, God already wired you for one. The same God that brought together and joined the first man and his wife is the same yesterday, today, and forever, and has a plan in place for everyone.

Raina and Angus

While in college and even after her first job, Raina was purposeful; she would spend time praying and was an inspiration to many young people in her circles. However, Raina became agitated a year before turning thirty because she was not yet married. Raina was not desperate to be married to just anyone but was prepared to wait until God sent her a man after His heart. Yet, she could not resist the pressure of feeling that no one had noticed her. Her mum encouraged her to be patient. Barely two years after Raina resumed work as the procurement lead in a start-up, she was asked to head a new office in another town. She reluctantly moved away from family and friends to begin life in a new community some sixty miles away from home. With this new position, and an apartment close to the office, she would not have to leave so early for work.

Raina began to jog each morning for half an hour before heading to work. Angus, who lived a few blocks away in the same community, also jogged in the morning, and soon they chat briefly before setting off on their run together. They enjoyed each other's company. Raina and Angus discovered that they had quite a bit in common, and since she was new to the area, Angus invited her to his church. Their friendship quickly morphed into a strong relationship. They were engaged in no time. Raina felt like she was watching a script play out.

While they were planning their wedding, Angus' office was closed in the town, and he had to move to another location. Raina was distraught; it had taken so long to get to this point in their relationship, and the person she had hoped would be her husband was now leaving town. How would they sustain a long-distance relationship? Had God indeed called them together? They put their wedding plans on hold to figure out the next steps, residing in different cities over the months that would follow. Raina continued to ask God for direction for the future. One day, while at work, she received a call from Angus. He was resigning to start up his company and moving back to the community where Raina lived. This was an answer to her prayers. During the trying months, Raina had grown closer to the Lord and was convinced in her heart that Angus was the one God had for her. With Angus away, she spent more time in prayer and the study of God's word. Things began to fall into place; it could have only been God. They got married some months after Angus moved back.

> Based on the principle of divine activity, God already has a best-selling book written, with your name as the title and with you as the main character.

"God works all things together for the good of them that love Him." Abraham, the father of faith, loved God and believed that the God he served would lead his servant to find the wife for his son. Abraham had experienced what God could do in his and Sarah's life. He knew that God was reliable. As in the prologue, Abraham assured the servant that God's angel would go before him: *For the Lord, the God of heaven, who took me from my father's house and my native land, solemnly promised to give this land to my descendants. He will send his angel ahead of you, and he will see to it that you find a wife there for my son.*[11] He had confidence in things he could not see.

Abraham assured his servant that the Divine would supply angelic help for finding the wife and indeed for every stage of fulfilling his purpose and in every season of life. Abraham was sure that God who appeared to him, who made promises to him and blessed him beyond his imagination, would undoubtedly have a wife for his son Isaac. Abraham's servant also showed his confidence in the God of his master as he embarked on the search. If you cared to reflect on it, you would realize that the Creator has led you all your life, even when life was at its toughest, even when you did not follow His promptings. And if you allow Him, He will also show you the spouse for you. God is the perfect matchmaker.

We listen to stories and paint pictures in our minds of the many ways our lives could play out. However, I have heard it said, that the most important story is the one you tell yourself. Above all the voices within and without, are you convinced that there is an ultimate plan for you? David said: '*You saw me before I was born. Every day of my life was recorded in your book. Every moment was laid out before a single day had passed.*'[12] This is the same for your life and mine since God is not partial[13].

Abraham's acknowledgment of God in the search for a wife is an application of the principle of divine activity. The principle of divine activity implies that your Creator has a bestselling book already written with your name as the title and with you as the star and main character. The principle of divine activity implies that you are convinced that God has a plan for your life beyond doubt. You need to step out each day, knowing that God orders your steps and that He will lead you to the spouse He has intended for you at the appointed time.

Divine activity releases power

Just as an apple tree would produce fruits that will have to mature at a certain time before they are ready to be eaten, Isaac's marriage would happen at the right time. Marriage was the next step for Isaac, and the family knew it was something God would help them with, just as He did with other issues. Abraham had raised his son Isaac and prepared him to lead his family and carry on their extraordinary promise from God. Both knew God would work behind the scenes concerning Isaac's marriage.

Operating in the principle of divine activity acknowledges that the God of all flesh who is the Sovereign Lord and King of kings and who made the heavens, and the earth will not allow a single hair of your head to fall to the ground without His approval. Before you choose your spouse and to benefit from the principle of divine activity, you must acknowledge that there is a God who knows you more, and before you knew yourself: *Before I shaped you in the womb, I knew all about you. Before you saw the light of day, I had holy plans for you...*[14] It is vital to know that if marriage is God's intent and design for you, not your idea or desire for yourself, then the Originator has a plan for it: *And the Lord God said, it is not good that the man should be alone, I will make him an help meet for him...*[15] He has already planned to do it.

> Applying the principle of divine activity means that you do not spend your time worrying about who, when, where or how to marry, or about the resources to host a wedding or live a fulfilled life

Before you considered marriage, God knew you would need a partner

Realizing the role of divine activity in looking to find and keep the love of your life is humbling. Before you considered marriage, God knew you would need a partner. He does not want you to be lonely. When you rely on the principle of divine activity, you realize that God already knows whom you will marry. When you are not looking from His perspective, your vision may be blurred, and the lack of clarity becomes a burden in finding the one. However, that burden is God's. When God brought Eve to Adam, he could only exclaim, *'this is now bone of my bones and flesh of my flesh, for she was taken out of [me] man!'* [16] When you realize that the partner you are searching for is already a part of you, taken from you or vice versa – from the beginning, then your prayers and expectations will change.

The experience of many has shown that getting anxious, dating just anyone, drawing unnecessary attention to yourself, and several other things people do in search of a spouse are often counterproductive. Self-aggrandizing activities or self-projection do not increase the probability of finding your life partner. Usually, when you are not even thinking of it, you will meet the one God intended for you, and then the relationship begins then or later. So why worry and lose sleep over something you have little or no influence on? God knows all about you and is set to make perfect all that concerns you - if you will allow Him. Jesus said, *'That is why I tell you not to worry about everyday life… for your heavenly Father already knows all your needs.'* [17]

Instead of exploring different relationships, leaving a trail of hurt and broken hearts, disappointments, and unnecessary intimacy, you can rest - assured. You can spend time connecting with God who made you. God knows who's just right for you and the timing for your connection. Instead of getting anxious over to whom and when you will get married, you can become a friend of God, discovering yourself in Him so that you will understand or recognize the rib from where you were taken, or that was taken from you.

Acknowledging and working in the principle of divine activity, the sovereignty of God over life, means you have an absolute faith that the God who instituted marriage, created you, and put the desire for a relationship in you, has a partner for you. Considering divine activity signifies you want that one God designed for your life. Accepting divine activity implies that you must walk by faith. Faith is the 'currency' of the principle of divine activity.

Abraham is known as the father of faith simply because he believed in God despite all the odds he faced. It is the same faith or absolute confidence that Abraham had that you need to access God's plans for your life and marriage. Faith or trust in God to find your life partner always yields the desired result: *'And it is impossible to please God without faith. Anyone who wants to come to him must believe that God exists and that he rewards those who sincerely seek Him.'* [18] God will reward you with answers about whom to choose to marry when you come to Him, believing.

Walking in the principle of divine activity, the sovereignty of God over life will bring peace to your heart. This peace comes from a 'knowing' that you are engraved on the palms of His hands and all the issues in your life, including your situation, makeup, needs, strengths, weaknesses, future, past, present, indeed all the days and years of your life – are always before Him.[19] There is no need to fear. God feeds the birds and clothes flowers in the fields, His eyes are on the sparrow, and He is watching over you. He says that He is for you, who can be against you. He says that the one that finds a spouse has found something good,[20] then you are that good thing that is about to be found.

The principle of divine activity expects you to trust God and be convinced within yourself, that He will lead and direct you in every area of your life, not just marriage. You need this conviction as an anchor because life's experiences will try to challenge this truth. But never forget that God always keeps His part of the plan.

Can there be great relationships outside of Divine activity?

Can there be great relationships outside of Divine activity? The answer is yes and no. So many people speak of how great a relationship they have enjoyed with their special one and how it was just luck, their good judgment, or just because they were meant for each other - without an acknowledgment of divine activity. I am sure you know some as well. The truth is that when you live a centered life, when you live by God's principles and laws, with a pure heart, you are living like God and inadvertently operating in the principle of Divine activity. However, do not underscore the importance of an intentional relationship with God, especially when trying to find the right and lasting love of your life. This is especially true in our world, where there is so much competing for our attention with little or no time to connect with God. Moreover, in some of these 'famed' relationships that are not Divine centered, when you think you are looking at the greatest love story of all times, you wake up to the news of divorce for 'irreconcilable differences!'

Divine activity works irrespective of the religion you profess; He is the God of all flesh, even if the world chooses not to acknowledge Him. God proved His sovereignty and instituted marriage before any form of organized religion. God is the creator and owner of all ethnicities of the earth and will answer whoever calls on Him. Even for those who do not know Him by His name and as their Lord and Savior, Paul had this to say: *'When outsiders who have never heard of God's principle follow it more or less by instinct, they confirm its truth by their obedience. They show that God's principle is not something alien (it is universal), imposed on us from without, but woven into the very fabric of our creation.*

There is something deep within them that echoes God's yes and no, right and wrong. Their response to God's yes and no will become public knowledge on the day God makes his final decision about every man and woman.[21]. God is God of all. God made all things for His pleasure: *"for thou hast created all things, and for thy pleasure they are and were created.*[22]" He created you and me for a close friendship with Him, for good works that we would carry out while we live on earth, and successful marriage is one of such good works. *For we are God's masterpiece, He has created us anew in Christ Jesus, so we can do the good things he planned for us long ago.*[23]

> God reveals hidden things. God can show and lead you to the partner that is just right for you.

The principle of divine activity is about collaborating with God on your life's storyline. Could you be coming from a family with a history of divorce and broken relationships? Even with an ill-luck, a tainted past, or unpleasant family history, you can turn the tables around. You can rewrite your history or change the course of your destiny for good by your relationship with God: *Jabez who was more honorable than any of his brothers. His mother named him Jabez because his birth had been so painful. He was the one who prayed to the God of Israel, "Oh that you would bless me and expand my territory! Please be with me in all that I do, and keep me from all trouble and pain!" And God granted him his request.* [24]

My prayer is that you will choose the good works the Divine One originally destined for you and even if it were otherwise, as Jabez did, you can rewrite your story. Here's another man who did: *So Jacob was left alone. Then a man wrestled with him until dawn. When the man saw that he could not win against Jacob, he touched the socket of Jacob's hip so that it* was dislocated as they wrestled. Then the man said, "Let me go; it's almost dawn." But Jacob answered, "I won't let you go until you bless me." So the man asked him, what's your name?" "Jacob," he answered. The man said, "Your name will no longer be Jacob but Israel [He Struggles with God],, because you have struggled with God and with men—and you have won."[25]

You have the freedom to approach God

At every crossroads in life, you have the freedom to approach God. God gives you the liberty and the agency to choose your outcomes. God is looking for those who are willing to get all that He has in store for them. His eyes of favor are eager to bring great answers to the questions of your life: *For the eyes of the Lord search back and forth across the whole earth, looking for people whose hearts are perfect toward him, so that he can show his great power in helping them...."*[26]

God will guide you along life's windy journey to the destiny He has for you: *He will keep in perfect peace all those who trust in him, whose thoughts turn often to the Lord*[27]. He will guide you through His word: *Your words are a flashlight to light the path ahead of me and keep me from stumbling*[28]. The direction you should go and the decisions you should take will become clearer with each passing day. *But the path of the just is like the shining sun, that shines ever brighter unto the perfect day.*[29]

Chapter 3
The principle of prayer

For prayer is nothing else than being on terms of friendship with God.

-Saint Teresa of Avila

I prayed so hard (many times out of fear) when I wanted to get married. I just wanted to make the right choice, and my reasons may not be unique to me. I did not want to choose under pressure, please my parents, or marry for the wrong reasons. I fasted and prayed a lot. I desperately wanted to connect to God's plan for me. One of the perhaps foolish prayers I prayed was, God please show me who you want me to marry; even if it is to happen in five years' time, let me know who it will be now, then I will rest my case and focus on you. Well, that did not happen. If God showed me who it would be then, even though I may not have been ready, the next prayer point would have been 'God let it happen now, immediately – I will learn whatever I need to learn in the marriage.' God in His wisdom knows when and how to answer our prayers.

Nonetheless, is it not interesting that the servant, Eliezer sent to find a wife for Isaac prayed at several stops along the journey? His practice of prayer

> *The principle of prayer activates, promotes, stirs up, advances, and encourages divine action and intervention in your life.*

is significant, considering what he achieved in the end. The principle of prayer is linked to the principle of divine activity. Prayer moves the hand of the Divine One, who moves situations in your life, in this case, finding and choosing a life partner. Prayer is two-way communication between you and your Maker.

The principle of prayer activates divine activity. Prayer promotes, stirs up, advances, and encourages divine action and intervention in your life. Through prayer, you get heaven's attention. Prayer does not leave any situation the same way it found it. Your faith builds when you pray and believe in your heart that God hears and answers. Preferably, you pray because you have realized that all things are possible with God. Believing and engaging in effective prayer means that you connect with the One who will leave no stone unturned to ensure that every obstacle on the path of your finding the right one and joyfully enjoying marriage is removed.

Abraham was a man of prayer with several recorded conversations and encounters with God. Abraham had an army of servants he had trained, and he no doubt taught his servants to pray, or they learned by observing their master. Prayer played a prominent role in the mission of finding the wife for Isaac. Although Abraham had a covenant with God and had been assured of God's plans for his family –the man he sent on assignment to find a wife for his son did not take the principle of prayer for his specific mission for granted.

Abraham assured his servant that the God he served would lead him: *The Lord God of heaven ...who spoke to me and swore to me... He will send His angel before you, and you shall take a wife for my son from there[30]*. Abraham's words were positive. Your words and confessions are prayers since words are alive and are seeds before God: *Now tell them this: 'As surely as I live, declares the Lord, I will do to you the very things I heard you say[31]*. You cannot afford to make casual statements that are negative, pray different things, and get commensurate answers to the prayers. Do you find yourself saying, 'there are no good people out there,' or 'I'm never going to find the right one' and then go to pray that God should give you a good spouse?

When you pray

Abraham's servant, Eliezer called on God. He relied on praying to God as his primary strategy to direct his way. He asked for divine guidance: *The servant had the camels kneel outside the city by the well. It was evening, when the women would go out to draw water. Then he prayed, "LORD, God of my master Abraham, make me successful today. Show your kindness to Abraham"[32]*.

Because of the gravity of his assignment, he prayed that one of the girls who would come to the well would be the one. Eliezer prayed, stepped out in faith and action to achieve the goal. He waited, and in answer to prayer, one of the girls he met began to check all the boxes. As the events progressed, Eliezer talked to God some more: *The man knelt, bowing to the LORD with his face touching the ground. He said, "Praise the LORD, the God of my master Abraham. The LORD hasn't failed to be kind and faithful to my master. The LORD has led me on this trip to the home of my master's*

> More than changing God's mind on a matter, true prayer will draw you closer to God, change your life, and open your spiritual eyes to know who your true partner is.

relatives[33]. He sets an example for some positions for effective prayer. You can kneel and bow to the Lord; you can walk, stand, or lie down to pray.

With more progress, it seemed too good to be true. He asked to go to the prospective wife's home to meet her family. When he had stated the mission and her family accepted the proposal and that the marriage could go on, he bowed in a prayer of praise:

When Abraham's servant heard their answer, he bowed down to the ground and worshiped the Lord[34]. Abraham's servant lived a life of worship and prayer. It is not surprising that the results were outstanding. If you are wondering if it was truly a prayer that the servant prayed, he recounted this story to the girl's family: "*So today when I came to the spring, I prayed this prayer: 'O Lord, God of my master, Abraham, please give me success on this mission. See, I am standing here beside this spring. This is my request*[35].

Simply present your request

Prayers are requests made to God. When you apply the principle of divine activity, you are functioning from an assurance that God is the Author and Finisher of your faith and has a life partner for you. As you apply the principle of prayer, you are oiling the engines of your faith for clarity and revelation. In praying, you ask God for direction on which way to go. As you pray, your faith increases, things begin to fall in place; obstacles, trials, and errors are resolved. You knock chance and freak occurrences out of your path.

Your spouse could be someone close by whom you never noticed before or in another location. When I least expected it, I got a call from over 6,000 miles away from the man who would be my husband. I would never have guessed that this would be the path to the initiation of my marriage. After we connected and with prayers, I got more clarity about the relationship, even though I could not influence the timing. Prayer will open your eyes to notice otherwise obscure but significant things that need your attention. When you pray, you are laying your burden at His feet. When you pray, you choose not to worry: *Don't worry about anything; instead, pray about everything. Tell God what you need and thank him for all he has done*[36].

Isaac, the prospective bridegroom, also walked in the principle of prayer. While the servant was out in search of the spouse, Isaac meditated, seeking God's face, praying that nothing short of God's best plan would evolve from the mission: *Isaac had just come back from Beer La hai Roi, since he was living in the Negev. Toward evening, Isaac went out into the field to meditate*[37]. It was his way of life. Times of quiet and meditation are manners of effective prayer. In *Pilgrim's Progress*, John Bunyan wrote, 'In prayer, it is better to have a heart without words than words without a heart.' While meditating, you are thinking over, musing, and coming to terms with God on His plans for your life or the issues at hand. According to Saint Francis de Sales, '*Half an hour's meditation each day is essential, except when you are busy. Then a full hour is needed.*' The higher the stakes, the more time you need to engage God.

Nneka and Lucas

Nneka had attended a marriage conference while she was in college. One of the speakers encouraged those attending to pray for their future spouses as early as possible. The speaker said he began to pray for his spouse many years before they got married and can attest that they have had no conflicts. Nneka was surprised as she had never heard of an utterly peaceful marriage, so she decided to take up the challenge. She did not want just any spouse but whomever God had planned. Nneka had a shortlist each time she prayed about a spouse; she wanted a godly, humble, and teachable spouse and got more than she prayed for. Lucas worked for the same company as her but in a different location. They met at the company's diversity workshop, where they sat beside each other. During one of the breakout sessions, they chatted and exchanged phone numbers. They had no clue they would get married someday.

Nneka was not sure if Lucas was single and so she did not keep in touch after the meeting as she said she would. Six months later, they met at another company meeting. Lucas would call Nneka, and then their friendship began. Lucas said he had been praying about Nneka since he met her and did not want to speak to her until he was sure she was the one. Nneka had been praying for a spouse and although her mind flashed on how friendly Lucas was, she did not think along those lines about him. After Lucas shared his intentions with her, he convinced her to keep praying that God would help them work things out.

Nneka was hesitant to commit to a relationship with Lucas but kept praying for direction for the future. A few weeks later, early one morning, Lucas called to announce his move to a new job at another location; she listened quietly to him and then shared her news with him as well. She had been moved to the exact location but was not considering it. They were both elated. Lucas asked Nneka if she would marry him, but she refused to respond on the phone. She continued to pray about all that happened, asking God to direct and lead. They got married shortly after and settled into their new location.

Nneka and Lucas have been married for almost seven years, and she describes her marriage as heaven on earth. She is so glad to be married to a godly, humble, and teachable man. Lucas has been a great spouse, the man of her dreams, and a role model besides. They have a great marriage, which they believe is a result of many years of praying.

God knows the end from the beginning

Jacob prayed a lot when he left his home to pursue his destiny. He even made a vow to God that he would make good if God answered his prayers and guided him. The outcomes of his life showed that God did indeed answer. Jacob met Rachel and fell head over heels in love with her. He was ready to sacrifice seven years of his life for her and did. However, Laban presented Leah to him in apparent deceit despite all of Jacob's efforts. Jacob was so disappointed and never quite loved Leah the way he loved Rachel, even after Rachel died. Yet in the end, Leah was the one that bore most of the sons that would extend the lineage, including Judah, the forebear of David and the Savior Jesus. The covenant was to be fulfilled through Leah, but Jacob wanted Rachel. Although Jacob struggled with this original purpose for the relationship that would shape the future, his prayers inadvertently guided and shaped his destiny. God knew that the covenant was with Leah and put her in Jacob's life. God knows the end from the beginning.

> *Prayer is a safety net that protects you from wrong decisions. You awaken your instincts to discern which way to go even when you can't point to the reason why.*

Beyond changing God's mind on any matter (such as praying that God would select a specific person to be your spouse), the essence of praying is that you draw closer to God and are changed in the process. Prayer will open your spiritual eyes to know God's direction for your life. Prayer will make your heart tender. You become a better person when you pray because you encounter the good and holy God. Prayer prepares you to be that desirable spouse who will be exactly right for your partner. Prayer will steer you in the direction to choose what God wants for you, which is best for you, not what you want for yourself – that may often not be the best in the end. Prayer strengthens you and equips you to withstand the storms of life and make the best of your marriage.

When you walk by the principle of prayer, you connect your spirit to the unseen realm, which is usually more than what is known or what you can feel, touch or taste: *For* God is Spirit, *so those who worship him must worship in* spirit ...[38]. You are awakened to discern which way to go, even when you cannot figure out why you are making those choices. Do you sense a strong desire to get married, or are you mature for marriage, or has someone signified their interest in beginning a relationship with you or vice versa? If that is the case, it's time to start a season of intense prayer and to study more of God's word. Before choosing the one, spend quality time in prayer (and after you get married, to keep the one!). Prayer is a safety net that protects you from potentially wrong decisions.

Jesus also told a story about a persistent widow that got her situation turned around to show that people should always pray and never give up.[39] When Jesus visited the coasts of Tyre and Sidon, he met a woman of Canaan, and she asked Him to heal her daughter who had an unclean spirit, but Jesus told her he had only come for the lost sheep of Israel. Her persistent prayer and faith moved Him to grant her request[40]. Prayer moves God to action.

Daniel prayed, and God answered his prayer; however, demonic forces delayed the answer for twenty-one days: *Then he said, "Don't be afraid, Daniel. Since the first day, you began to pray for understanding and to humble yourself before your God; your request has been heard in heaven. I have come in answer to your prayer. But for twenty-one days, the spirit prince of the kingdom of Persia blocked my way. Then Michael, one of the archangels, came to help me*[41]. Satan got in the way of the answer from God. Daniel did not know all these, but he continued in prayer, and God sent a more powerful angel to deliver the answer to his prayer. The superheroes in the movies seem to understand all too well the spiritual realm's activities. Resistance and opposition to a purpose beyond what is physically visible happens. Because you do not understand the activities in the spiritual realm over your life or what battles are being fought over your destiny, prayer becomes necessary. It is commonly said that a prayer-less person is a powerless person.

In addition to prayers, consider fasting. Fasting weakens the flesh and strengthens your spirit so that you are more sensitive to hearing from God. You must pray until you are sure God is leading you on a particular path. As you talk to God regularly in prayer, you will begin to know His voice. Just as easy as it is to be able to identify your friends' voices when they call, you will grow to recognize God's voice by your frequent communication with Him. And as you obey His instructions, you will grow spiritually. His Spirit will lead you as you spend quality time with Him regularly.

Chapter 4
The principle of the assignment

"I knew you before I formed you in your mother's womb. Before you were born, I set you apart and appointed you as my prophet to the nations."

Jeremiah 1: 5 NLT

Shade and Lanre

Shade and Lanre had been dating for over seven years. Her family and friends were sure they would get married. Shade waited forever for Lanre to pop the question, but he never did. He had become a part of her life with no commitments. They were intimate, but it appeared their relationship was going nowhere. Even though they had become an item among their friends, Lanre was not keen on getting married just yet.

While at dinner one day, Shade asked Lanre a question she had been dreading, 'what are your expectations for our relationship'? She was appalled when he said she had met all his expectations but that he was watching to see how the relationship would unfold. Marriage was not on his radar now. That did not make much sense to her - after seven years. The following week she told him she was not going to wait and see what would happen to them. She was moving on and would not keep hanging out with a person who had no sense of direction about his life or their relationship. After their relationship ended, Shade began a journey to seek God and discover His assignment for her life. She was sad that she had lost those years hanging on to Lanre. Lanre never challenged her to restore the relationship. Like a rudderless ship, their long relationship had been drifting with no direction.

Shade decided she would not get into any relationship for at least another year. Even when a few people expressed their interest, she turned down the offers. She began to fast and pray and studied God's word, grateful that her relationship with Lanre was over. She overcame the need to be seen as being hooked up. She realized that Lanre never encouraged her relationship with God or shared her passion for serving God. Her relationship with him had robbed her of many of her core values. She had made many compromises to keep him. She decided that her next and final relationship would be with purpose, with her life partner. They would establish ground rules and discuss their expectations early on.

Shade began to focus on her tasks at work and put in extra hours to keep herself busy. Almost a year after ending her relationship with Lanre, while working late one day, she met Chidera, a young man automating systems for her company. Chidera was frequent at the office, and they began to chat and quickly became good friends. Closing at work together became a regular occurrence. They found they shared the same values and faith. As the relationship grew, Shade and Chidera got married. Shade would have continued to hang out with Lanre with no end in view had she not summoned the courage to ask the pertinent question over dinner. She would have missed the opportunity of a lifetime to partner with Chidera.

The assignment

From the beginning, God had a mandate for each person He created, over seven billion of us, at the time of writing of this book: *Then God blessed them, and God said to them, "Be fruitful and multiply; fill the earth and subdue it; have dominion over the fish of the sea, over the birds of the air, and over every living thing that moves on the earth."*[42] This is our overall assignment.

Then the Lord God took the man and put him in the Garden of Eden to tend and keep it.[43] This was Adam's specific assignment. God has a purpose and mission for every man and woman He created. No one is on planet earth without a mission from God. You only need to discover or come to the realization of it. God placed the man in the Garden of Eden to 'dress and keep' it. God gave the man an assignment in a location. He was not to be idle. As God observed the man carrying out his assignment in the garden, He saw that the man was alone and needed someone suitable to help him: *Now the Lord God said, It is not good (sufficient, satisfactory) that the man should be alone; I will make him a helper (suitable, adapted, complementary) for him.*[44] It was for the success of the assignment that God decided that Adam needed a spouse.

Therefore, Adam's assignment was first, then the requirement for a helpmate came next. The man had a purpose and a task for being. He had a mission to accomplish on earth. He was to be fruitful in it, multiply, replenish, subdue, and have dominion over the earth as he fulfilled his assignment.

Eliezer, while declaring his mission to the prospective spouse's family, defined who his master was: *"I am Abraham's servant,"* he explained. *"And Jehovah has overwhelmed my master with blessings so that he is a great man among the people of his land. God has given him flocks of sheep and herds of cattle, and a fortune in silver and gold, and many slaves and camels and donkeys. Now when Sarah, my master's wife, was very old, she gave birth to my master's son, and my master has given him everything he owns."*[45] He refers to Abraham as a great man among the people, a person of influence, a leader. Abraham was also a wealthy man who had given everything he owned to his son, Isaac. What an enormous responsibility for Isaac, and how blessed he was.

Besides the material inheritance Abraham left for his son, he passed on the spiritual mantle, the covenant, and the assignment he had from God to build him a nation of believers. This assignment was going to be a lifetime project for Isaac. Isaac handed this assignment to his children when he blessed them with the mandate and every subsequent generation since then has had this sense of purpose and assignment from God. Isaac was a man on a mission. He was not an idle man seeking a wife.

You have an assignment

Jesus told the parable of a ruler that divided life tasks or talents among his servants to trade with until he returned: *"For the kingdom of heaven is like a man traveling to a far country, who called his own servants and delivered his goods to them. And to one he gave five talents, to another two, and to another one, to each according to his own ability; and immediately he went on a journey."*[46] There is an assignment that God has given you to accomplish, which you must strive toward, daily. Ask yourself, 'What has God put in my life that I must trade with and give account to Him in the end?'

Before you embark on finding and choosing the one, ask yourself - Do I know my life's purpose? Have I discovered my assignment on earth? Which 'garden' has the Lord asked me to tend, or which garden have I been equipped to help to tend? What is my assignment? What is my purpose and mission in life? What is that deep hunger of my heart, no holds barred?

If you have discovered your purpose, how are you going about fulfilling your assignment? Are you at the preparatory stage? Have you already started on your life assignment? Are you at the beginning or end of a particular phase of your life? If an individual does not know the purpose for their life or at least some of it (since we evolve in our assignments), there will be confusion because they will not appreciate the help meet sent into their lives. A lack of knowledge of one's assignment in life before marriage creates a vacuum that breeds dissatisfaction that festers in the relationship. Your life's assignment is not necessarily your job or your means of income. Your occupation may not be your vocation, even though they could be the same in some cases.

> The principle of the assignment states that before God gave man a helpmeet for him, He gave him an 'assignment', a purpose for his life and He equipped his woman to be suitable, adapted, and right for him.

Isaac, the prospective groom, had his 'garden to tend and keep.' Isaac was a wealthy rancher, effectively managing the wealth left to him by his father, Abraham. His assignment was connected to God's call on his father, Abraham - to raise a nation for God. He had come to accept the weighty covenant his father had with God and was a full partner committed to continuing their family's call of birthing a nation for God.

Abraham's servant said: *"The Lord has blessed my master abundantly, and he has become wealthy. He has given him sheep and cattle, silver and gold, male and female servants, and camels and donkeys. My master's wife Sarah has borne him a son in her old age, and he has given him everything he owns.*[47] Another reference states that: *Abraham left everything he owned to Isaac.*[48] Besides the physical inheritance, Isaac also received the promise of God to Abraham *'that all the nations will be blessed through him.'*[49]. Even though he had an inheritance, he labored in his purpose. He was industrious, and he grew to become a great businessman in his own right: *Isaac planted crops in that land and the same year reaped a hundredfold, because the* LORD *blessed him. The man became rich, and his wealth continued to grow until he became very wealthy. He had so many flocks and herds and servants that the Philistines envied him.*[50]

While money and possessions are essential aspects of the principle of the assignment, they represent only a type of outcome of the principle, but they are not the only ones. The principle of the assignment is also seen in terms of lives transformed, impact to development, peace, and progress in a setting. In any case, marriage would require resources – material and immaterial; you will need to be engaged in your assignment and employ your whole being to sustain your relationship.

The apostle Paul said that *'Anyone who does not provide for their relatives, and especially for their own household, has denied the faith and is worse than an unbeliever.'* [51] While your assignment will bring you rewards that enable you to provide for your home, it starts with discovering your purpose in life, pursuing it, excelling, and prospering in it. There must be a sense of direction or advancement in purpose, especially for the man, if he wants to be the true leader of the union.

A woman's purpose

What about the woman? Does she have a purpose? Does she have an assignment? Yes. The original mandate was given to the man and woman at creation. He made them "male and female" and handed the earth to them to steward. People often ask, "If a woman's purpose is to help the man fulfill his purpose, does she then not have her assignment from God?" Is there a chance that a woman's purpose is not connected to the man's assignment who is interested in her? Should a woman abandon her perceived assignment for her husband? How exactly is the concept of the help meet defined in our context today? First, it is safe to say that there will be an agreement of purpose when a man finds the spouse that God has chosen for him. *'The woman was created for the man.'*[52] Considering all that a woman invests first in herself, in her marriage and the sacrifices most women and their families make to become who they are, women stuck in troubled and strained marriages will not want to hear that they have been created for their husbands. It may sound archaic or selfish, but as the helper, a woman's intellect, material, and spiritual gifts should ultimately work to help her husband fulfill their overall assignment.

In marriage, a man's and his wife's purpose are intertwined, but not necessarily in terms of the same vocation. They are to have a oneness of heart toward

The principle of the assignment is more about discovering your purpose in life, pursuing it, excelling, and prospering in it.

their reason for existence and their collective impact in the world - starting from their immediate family. In addition to the favor she brings, a wife adds value to their shared destiny: *The man who finds a wife finds a treasure, and he receives favor from the Lord.* [53]

Before I got married, I was inspired to write in my journal that my mission in life is to assist people to fulfill their destinies. I did not fully understand the meaning then or how it would happen, but looking back, I can see that I easily supported or helped people around me.

During our pre-marital counseling, we were asked to define what we perceived our joint assignment in life to be. It was incredible what we wrote individually, how we combined both to create a shared vision, how life has merged our purposes, and how everything has turned out over the years. We have a lot of unity regarding the purpose and direction of our lives, even when we have different views of how we should go about it.

I have a friend who is a gifted and accomplished musician. At some point, he complained to me that his love interest was not in any way interested in the object of his passion. She had never attended any of his shows and never asked about his work or music ministry. He worried that she did not go out of her way to watch him perform and that he did not want to force it, yet he was so attracted to her. He was concerned about going forward with the relationship as it appeared to be a red flag that there was no alignment in their assignments. What do you think? How would you feel living the rest of your life with someone who does not take any interest at all in what you do? Would that matter to you?

In the prologue, we see that Rebekah was actively about her assignment when Abraham's servant saw her: *See, I am standing here beside this spring, and the young women of the town are coming out to draw water ... Before he had finished praying, he saw a young woman named Rebekah coming out with her water jug on her shoulder.*[54] He found her at her 'assignment,' serving her family's business. In addition, when Rachel was 'found' by Jacob, she was actively engaged with her assignment, which may have been her vocation: *Jacob was still talking with them when Rachel arrived with her father's flock, for she was a shepherd.*[55] She was a professional. She took care of the sheep, fed them, helped them calve, protected them, treated their illnesses, and much more. Jacob eventually married Rachel, who was of his same vocation.

Another favorite Bible character is Ruth, also a woman on assignment. Ruth had just returned to Israel with her mother-in-law, Naomi. She had recognized that her assignment in that season of her life was to stay close by, love, and take care of the devastated widow who had lost her husband and two sons. Ruth had a selfless heart that looked beyond her immediate needs and pleasures to attend to Naomi's welfare. Moreover, while she cared for Naomi during those years,

Discovering your assignment, understanding it, and walking in it, increases your possibility of choosing the right partner

she found time to work outside the home to support and provide for the two of them. She asked herself, 'what can I do to enable me to fulfill my purpose of serving this woman Naomi?'

Perhaps she evaluated the situation. What can I do in this season to get me ready for where I want to go? "What gifts do I have? What do I have to offer? What do I enjoy doing?" She stepped out and started with the first work she found: *Whatever your hand finds to do, do it with all your strength. For there is no work or planning or learning or wisdom in the place of the dead where you are going.* [56] There birthed a vocation, a secondary assignment, in response to the original need.

Initially, she got busy serving Naomi, and then started a job so that she and Naomi would not die of hunger: *One day Ruth the Moabite said to Naomi, "Let me go out into the harvest fields to pick up the stalks of grain left behind by anyone who is kind enough to let me do it." Naomi replied, "All right, my daughter, go ahead." So Ruth went out to gather grain behind the harvesters. And as it happened, she found herself working in a field that belonged to Boaz, the relative of her father-in-principle, Elimelech*[57]. She started from where she was. Ruth was actively involved in her assignments in that season when she 'coincidentally' came to the business place of Boaz, who would eventually marry her. Her assignment and purpose would evolve to her becoming a wife to Boaz, a mother, and to being available to be used to prepare the lineage of the Messiah.

There is a common thread in the lives of these women. They were 'found' for marriage while they were about their assignment, and not necessarily in the sense of a physical location. Funnily enough, Rahab, the prostitute, married an Israelite man (whom theologians argue was one of the spies sent to Jericho) that she hid on her roof. She supported a mission for God from her infamous work, saved her family, and became relevant in history. Who knows what conditions led her into prostitution? She had a noble heart and may have been looking for a way out, and the opportunity came. She was on her 'assignment,' being a savior of sorts while hiding the spies, [58] through whom she saved her whole family when Jericho was destroyed. She is named to the lineage of Christ. There is a chance that the spies may have asked other women on those walls to help them, but they refused and instead reported to the king's men, which may have led to the search for the spies?

While the servant was about his assignment for Abraham, he found the one. It was easier for God to lead him in the 'way,' being in the path: The KJV version says it best: And he said, *"Blessed be the Lord God of my master Abraham, who hath not left destitute my master from His mercy and His truth. I, being on the way, the Lord led me to the house of my master's brethren."* As a man or woman, you may not have discovered your assignment, or fully understand it, or be about, but be in the way of it. There may be no results to show for what God has given to you to be or do, but you must live in the consciousness of it, that you are here on purpose. Your assignment could be as simple as being a mother or father who raised godly children. No assignment is trivial, no matter how simple it may sound.

> These women appear to have been 'found' for marriage while going about their purpose or while they were about their assignment.

Who writes the job description for the assignment?

God gave Adam the assignment of tending the garden, but Adam did not know he would need a help meet. God saw the need and subsequently created the woman and called her a 'help meet.' God gave the woman her assignment. God knows best what He called the woman to do in her man's life –it is not for the man or woman to necessarily decide the type of help they need or the assignment for the other. So, truly one cannot develop a description of the personality, qualifications, qualities, gifts, or career their prospective spouse should have.

The way your assignment plays out today may not be the same in ten years. Your assignment may not be in synchrony with your occupation now. We often think people in similar jobs would be great for each other, but it does not always turn out that way. "I am a doctor, I will find a hard-working nurse to marry, and we will build the clinic of my dreams." Your wife may not necessarily share the same dream or be equipped to work best with you. Many discover after college that God had called them to do something entirely different from what they studied and proceed to pursue other passions, not in line with their discipline.

Each person must strive to understand their assignment in life. You will need to seek the Father's face and know what He has wired and called you to do, and then both of you as a prospective couple must seek to understand why God brought you together. A spouse can only be effective to the extent that they are suited for the assignment God has given their partner. God has a unique job description for each person in their relationship. You cannot wish for your spouse to be or function as a person or role that they are not.

There are many ways to discover your assignment. Your assignment may be given to you straight from heaven, as in the case of Moses, Jeremiah, or Paul, who said that they had a direct call from God defining the course of their lives. Your assignment could be the desires and burdens God lays on your heart. The news about the ruins in Jerusalem pained Nehemiah, and he desired to go and rebuild the city. He did not claim to hear an audible voice asking him to do so. Your assignment can be thrust on you by the experiences and circumstances you find yourself in, and you will be compelled to rise to the occasion.

Talk to God in prayer about your purpose. If you are sincere and committed to doing what God wants you to do, He will lead you and steer you on the right path. He will close the wrong doors when you are confused. The plans and purposes of God for your life are for a lifetime. You will always need to grow into your assignment. He may give you the big picture at once, or He may reveal your assignment in bits that you can handle as you walk with Him every day.

Every assignment has a set of outcomes; every labor has a reward. There is a place and path to the fulfillment of your assignment. When you discover your assignment, you gain a sense of direction, the path for your life. You are constantly propelled along a specific path by the divine vision in your mind, giving direction to your life. Each route you take in life has a focus and specific type of people, and hopefully, your spouse is also walking that path (however, be careful of the counterfeits, the wolves in sheep clothing who get on your path in error). There will be high and low moments in your assignment, but keep at it.

When your assignment is clear, you will have a vision of the result. God asked Habakkuk to write the vision to stir up a response: *And the Lord said to me, "Write my answer on a billboard, large and clear, so that anyone can read it at a glance and rush to tell the others.*[59] Another version says, 'that he may run that reads it.' Vision attracts people of like minds, like values. People that identify with your vision respond and want to act. Vision is a recruiter.

Values are beliefs that guide your life and put you on specific paths of travel in life. Some preferred values for relationships include integrity, courage, punctuality, family relationships, and loyalty. These values go hand in hand to help you fulfill your vision. Your values are developed from your family, education, religion, culture, or community. The best source of right values is the word of God, His precepts. Your values play an essential role in helping you discover and fulfill your assignment in life and ultimately choosing a spouse.

Values are like ladders leaning on the wall that you climb on the path of your destiny. First, the ladder must be leaning on the right walls, and the base and foundation must be strong enough. In workshops, I usually ask participants to list three people they admire most in life and give a reason or two why they admire them so much. When you can articulate what you admire most in your heroes, you are not far from identifying the values you hold dear. The explanations for why you admire or want to be like the persons you admire are likely the most substantial values that resonate with you and that you have or desire. Check, if these values are not foundational to the outcomes you would like in life and marriage, then you can either review or change them.

The principle of the assignment is crucial in choosing a life partner. In summary, the principle states that before God gave the man help meet for him, or before he gave the woman as a wife to the man, He gave him an 'assignment,' a purpose for his life. He equipped her to be suitable, adapted, and exactly right for him. Discovering your assignment, understanding it, and living it, will enable you to choose the right partner and build a working marriage. Abraham's son, Isaac, was actively involved in his family's assignment of raising a people for God. Though he had an immediate occupation or vocation to support his family, that was his primary mission. As we saw in the prologue, when Rebekah's family blessed her, it was with the same blessing guiding Isaac's purpose, although they were not there when Abraham and Isaac received their call. There, their alignment lay.

The provisions and blessings are tied to your assignment and the vision for your life. The fortune of Abraham belonged to Isaac. He was well-resourced for his marriage. As you walk in your assignment, the provisions, fortune, and blessings for your life and marriage will be abundantly available to you. You may not discover all your purpose at once, but if your heart is inclined to seek and find God's plans, you will see a pattern emerge that could only have been divinely orchestrated.

Chapter 5
The principle of timing

"For everything there is a season, a time for every activity under heaven.[60]

Chichi would graduate from college in a year. Over the long holidays, she enrolled as an intern in a small consulting firm. She met Obi at lunch in the first few weeks after she resumed. Obi did not hide that he was interested in a relationship; it was love at first sight. They would meet for lunch regularly, and what began as an off-the-cuff relationship fast-tracked into an intensely passionate relationship neither of them could manage. Barely two months after she started her internship, Chichi became pregnant. Because of her values, abortion was out of the question. Her parents were disappointed and could not understand how she got herself into this mess. She completed her internship but could not return for her final year in college. She and Obi decided she should move in with him and his parents.

Both families agreed to a hurried civil marriage. Chichi had her baby but still could not return to school because they could not afford care for the baby. Obi's behavior towards her changed drastically, and she became a slave of sorts living with his parents. They both continued to live with Obi's parents for the next three years. Disagreement and arguments were frequent. Obi wanted more children, but Chichi was not happy with her situation and so would not consider it. Intimacy was stalled and led to significant conflict. Going back to school was a priority for Chichi. Still, Obi thought it would not add any value, would not support her, and wanted her to have more children for him instead, almost as payment for 'the sacrifice' his family made, to take away her shame, and to have him marry her.

Chichi and Obi are finally moving out of the family house and to their own home, with their third daughter on the way. Chichi is a shadow of herself, regrets meeting Obi, and thinks of divorce each day. But she is also worried about a future for her girls without a father figure. There are nights Obi would not return home. Her life seems to be on pause as she wonders how she got herself in this situation. She had been distracted by the false hopes and promises of undying love from Obi. She had not taken time to understand his values before getting entangled with him. With the children and their needs in tow, how would she go back to graduate and make a life for herself? She is working to mend the fantastic relationship she had enjoyed with her parents. Is there a chance she can regain all the opportunities that once lay ahead? She is desperate to work herself out of the many poor choices.

Neither Chichi nor Obi was ready to get married - she was naïve, immature, and pressured by passion. She had hoped that their relationship would evolve, that he would wait for her to complete her studies, but unfortunately, everything went south, fast. Chichi thought she had met the man of her dreams who genuinely loved her, but Obi was not thinking long-term when he met her. These two young adults with different perspectives on life and different expectations from each other will now manage the challenges of marriage and parenting while they face an uncertain future.

A time to get married

If there is a season for everything and every purpose under heaven, then there is a time to get married and a time to be single. There is a time to be in a relationship and a time not to be in one. At creation, there came a time when God decided to create Adam, and at another time, God gave him an assignment. Then, at another time, as Adam worked at the task God gave him, God decided Adam would need a helper.

There is an opportune time to get married. God has planned out your life in times and seasons. The stages of life - birth, childhood, youth, adulthood, old age, and eventually death signifies the changing seasons and have their unique features and demands. You will move from one stage to another - no one is here forever. The days of your life are written in a book. God has a script for each person. *'You saw me before I was born. Every day of my life was recorded in your book. Every moment was laid out before a single day had passed.'*[61]

Not everyone has this conviction about their lives, but that is how it is. It is essential to be at peace with each stage of your life and not allow yourself to be constantly worried about the next thing. What is the season of your life now? Should you be in school or a learning system preparing for your destiny? Are you in your learning, earning, or resting phase of life? Is it time to get married? Are you prepared and ready for marriage? Are you concerned about your age, thinking you are running out of time? God's timing is not the same as ours. God is not constrained or controlled by time. He created time, but He lives in eternity: *With the Lord a day is like a thousand years, and a thousand years are like a day.*[62]

God knows your times. He determined the number of eggs in a woman's ovary, which will not be there forever. Yet, He could make Sarah have a child – when she was told her eggs were no longer viable and could bless families with children that are not biologically theirs. He is faithful and able.

At the herald of every season of your life, if you listen closely, you will hear the gentle signals. Solomon said, '*Yet God has made everything beautiful for its own time. He has planted eternity in the human heart, but even so, people cannot see the whole scope of God's work from beginning to end.*'[63] If you take the time to listen to your heart, you will understand your times. *Your own ears will hear him. Right behind you a voice will say, "This is the way you should go," whether to the right or to the left.*[64]

When the time had come for Isaac to get married, his family knew that the next step was to find a suitable wife. They had learned that in God's time, the provision required would be available.

Understanding time

As Solomon wrote, the LORD is a God of times and seasons. Every activity under heaven has an ideal time. It is easy to become involved in your purposes ahead of or later than their perfect timing. The ability to understand the times and seasons is a grace. The men of the tribe of Issachar were described as those that '*understood the signs of the times and knew the best course for Israel to take.*'[65] That is an important aspiration for success in every area of life. Right timing is essential in finding or choosing your spouse.

The significance of timing was obvious as Eliezer searched for a wife for his master's son. At the secondary level, the servant started and arrived at the well at a specific time: *Then the servant took ten of his master's camels and departed, for all his master's goods were in his hand. And he arose and went to Mesopotamia, to the city of Nahor. And he made his camels kneel down outside the city by a well of water at evening time, the time when women go out to draw water.*[66] It was the time the women would come to the well, being about their business. That the servant got to the well at a specific time to begin his assignment is in itself profound. Similar timing-related incidents occurred when Jacob arrived at the well and met Rachel or when Ruth unknowingly gleaned in Boaz's farm at that time and season. These appeared to be like coincidences. But God orders or directs the path of those who are committed to Him: *The Lord directs the steps of the godly. He delights in every detail of their lives.*[67]

> The principle of timing implies that life is lived in times and seasons. There is a time to be seek and be found, a time for love, and a time to get married.

The principle of timing implies that life is lived in times and seasons. There is a time to be found, a time to love and be loved, a time to get married, and a time to end a marriage (hopefully not until death parts). Walking in the principle of timing implies that you must understand the seasons of your life. There is a time to be born, to grow, to learn, to earn, to multiply, and there is a time to rest. What time is it for you now?

Leading up to when I met my husband, I felt like I was the only one left of my friends who was not yet married. I was not that old, but many of my friends were already married, had begun to have children, and I foolishly wondered if there was anyone out there for me. Meanwhile, I was reading books about marriage, attending seminars, and thinking a lot about what it would take to have a good marriage. Those days, they were airing a musician, Nel Oliver's song Baby Girl, at almost every commercial break on the local TV. Tears welled up my eyes each time I watched the man give his daughter away in marriage. My parents were praying that I would make the right choice. I somehow knew at that time that both my parents and I were ready. Somehow, I just knew it was time.

Shortly afterward, I would encounter my husband. I was overseeing my parish's bookstore and church library. I would comb bookstores across town after I closed from work to find good books for the store. One of the books that caught my attention those days was *God's Generals* by Roberts Liardon. I probably sold, gifted, and talked about that book more than any other book I'd read in that season. One ordinary day, in my sister's home, the phone rang, and they said it was a call for me. There were no mobile phones then, so I had to go to the staircase to sit and talk. Who was it? John Enelamah! Johnny, or long John as friends called him then, was a family friend and had been three years my senior in high school. We barely spoke in school. I had this picture of a tall, lanky boy, wearing jump-up trousers (he was too tall for the regular-sized, school-supplied uniforms) and was always smiling during family visiting days. He was visiting with some mutual family friends in the Washington DC area who informed him that my parents were visiting my sister and her husband in Silver Spring. He went to see them, and of course, my name came up in the conversations, and he got my number from them.

I was surprised to receive his call, seemingly out of the blue. He told me he had just graduated from Spirit Life Bible College founded by Roberts Liardon. The author of *God's Generals?* My rave book of the

> To understand the times and seasons of your life, a close relationship with God is a prerequisite, via the principle of divine activity and prayer.

moment? You can tell he got my attention, and we would have a lot to discuss. The rest, as they say, is history.

The time and season for me to meet the one had come, and even though we were thousands of miles apart, God still found a way to connect us. What moved him to visit with these specific friends in Washington DC at that time? He had other friends who did not know my sister whom he could have stayed with on that trip. It was just the time.

To understand the times and seasons of your life, a close relationship with God is a prerequisite via the principle of divine activity and prayer. It is either you understand the seasons of your life for yourself, or you have the 'men of Issachar' (wise mentors) in your life who understand the pattern of your life and are available to pray, counsel, and point you in the right direction. I am not referring to friends or peers who may put you under pressure to get married at a particular time, for the wrong reasons, or insist on a specific kind of individual.

Age and biologically determined fertility span should not be the overriding reason to get married. Both men and women may come under pressure from people around them to commit to whosoever is available. After leaving college, many women look forward to getting married, and it could feel awkward when no one seems to be attracted to you. I went through a season where I had so much attention that my siblings began to call me 'stampede'. Then there was a long season when there seemed to be no one noticing me at all. Society and culture including yourself will want to make you feel old and forgotten. You must decide which culture you will live by - 'kingdom culture' which works with the timing of God for your marriage or 'society culture,' that uses stereotypes and man-made rules to put you under pressure and bondage to get married so that you are not seen as being alone. There is God's timing and season of response for your life. Do not put yourself under unnecessary pressure; your time to get married will come.

Old enough?

The principle of timing also relates to the maturity of persons who desire to get married. There is a time when a man's mind is mature enough to undertake the responsibility of leading both himself and a new family unit. *'A man shall leave his father and mother and be joined to his wife'*[68]. This statement is not referring to a boy or girl. Marriage is for a man and a woman. Also, for instance, *Rebekah was very beautiful and old enough to be married*[69]. 'Old enough' here speaks to maturity. There is a time when a man or a woman is mature, responsible, and ready for marriage. While age is just a number, some young people are ripe and ready for marriage even though they are chronologically young. At the same time, some adults you expect to be mature are very irresponsible and not prepared for marriage.

There are dire consequences of violating the timing principle, such as when young and immature people get married. These range from trauma, emotional unpreparedness for the issues in marriage to reproductive organs that become compromised. Further, many are yet to discover their purpose, and when they do many years later, these couples grow apart and begin to regret their choices when there is no alignment in their visions for the future.

Often, when a couple is attracted to each other, they want to get married almost immediately since they are so in love, feel pressured to do so, or because they or their parents have the means to give them a head start. There is nothing wrong with that stance; after all, Rebekah decided to marry Isaac immediately after meeting the emissary and the proposal - before sighting him. They did not embark on a six-month or two-year engagement. However, you must realize that Isaac and Rebekah both had a solid foundation, and their families were not quite strangers.

Their families shared the same values and beliefs, a crucial element in the journey to oneness in a marriage that bridged many gaps in their relationship.

It is advisable to plan on a healthy length of time for courtship based on the needs of your specific relationship. Some couples got married barely a month after meeting themselves and are doing very well. However, it is usually safer to spend more time praying and preparing for the marriage (not the wedding). Invest time to know more about your backgrounds and families and paint a realistic picture of your desired future together before committing. Time to build your relationship is more critical than ever as our world becomes more complex and transactions and interactions go digital. People are getting hooked up via online platforms and often present a 'doctored,' more pleasing image of themselves to the other. It takes time to know how much of the other's character and actions you can predict accurately and under various life situations. Someone may be perfect for you but be a work in progress. Over time you can understand their mindset, points of agreement, and areas that may be challenging in marriage. It is usually safer to work on these before the wedding or to decide whether you can spend the rest of your life living with that behavior or issue or not.

Do not rush into planning a wedding, no matter how much money you have, how you feel about each other, or how compatible

Let the principle of timing work for you, not against you, testing your integrity and character, bedrocks of any successful marriage.

you think you are with your prospective spouse. Except you are known to procrastinate or dilly dally with making important decisions, let your relationship evolve to a level that both of you are comfortable with. The two of you should articulate how you have grown as a couple in a relationship. There are many arguments over the ideal duration between meeting your prospective spouse and the right time to get married. Every relationship and context are unique.

On the other hand, do not extend your courtship unduly to find faults or discover something that could change your mind. You want to sort out any gray areas that could rob you of your peace and plan from the onset how you would work together as a team to manage differences you cannot change. It is usually more challenging to change these expectations after getting married.

The use of time

A massive test of the strength and purpose of a relationship sometimes happens when there are obstacles or delays in the marriage plans, and the couple needs to endure or wait. Here is Jacob's case: *Now Laban had two daughters. The older daughter was named Leah, and the younger one was Rachel. There was no sparkle in Leah's eyes, but Rachel had a beautiful figure and a lovely face. Since Jacob was in love with Rachel, he told her father, "I'll work for you for seven years if you'll give me Rachel, your younger daughter, as my wife." "Agreed!" Laban replied. "I'd rather give her to you than to anyone else. Stay and work with me." So, Jacob worked seven years to pay for Rachel. But his love for her was so strong that it seemed to him but a few days.*[70] Hello, that was some waiting!

Jacob and Rachel are an encouragement to couples who cannot get married for one reason or the other when they would like to. These are usually trying times for the relationship. For some, this could be a sign to let go. However, those who are

Love is the more reason why you can wait for love, and not the reason to be in a hurry and act in haste

meant to be and endure these trying seasons discover that a tried and tested friendship evolves. Do you know that after working so hard for seven years, Jacob still did not get the whole deal: *Finally, <u>the time came</u> for him to marry her. "I have fulfilled my agreement," Jacob said to Laban. "Now give me my wife so I can marry her." So Laban invited everyone in the neighborhood and prepared a wedding feast. But that night, when it was dark, Laban took Leah to Jacob, and he slept with her... But when Jacob woke up in the morning—it was Leah!*

"What have you done to me?" Jacob raged at Laban. "I worked seven years for Rachel! Why have you tricked me?" "It's not our custom here to marry off a younger daughter ahead of the firstborn," Laban replied. "But wait until the bridal week is over, then we'll give you Rachel, too—provided you promise to work another seven years for me." So, Jacob agreed to work seven more years. A week after Jacob had married Leah, Laban gave him Rachel, too... So, Jacob slept with Rachel, too, and he loved her much more than Leah. He then stayed and worked for Laban the additional seven years. [71]

Jacob loved Rachel and decided he would invest an additional seven years of his life working to get married to the love of his life - and yet his love for her did not wane. Another lesson from Jacob's use of time here is that your love for someone is the more reason you can wait for the relationship to mature, and not the reason to hurry and act in haste or insist on sexual intimacy. When you find yourself having to decide under pressure or in a hurry, for instance, insisting that a prospective spouse should respond to a proposal within a certain period or where you are issued an ultimatum - beware! The Bible says that he who believes shall not act hastily[72] and indeed, haste makes waste[73]. It is ok to ask for more time when you are unsure or not ready.

The test of time

Why do we place so much value on antiques and artwork from the past? Why is wine preserved for many years to taste better? The principle of timing is also about relationship decisions that stand the test of time. Timing empowers you to question that your choice in marriage is and will be God's best for you over the long haul. Before you commit to something as weighty as the decision to get married, do ask, 'Will this decision stand the test of time?' The passage of time will test and confirm the strength of your relationship before and after you embark on it.

Do not come under pressure regarding the specific date you will get married. Just because it is the beginning of a new year or almost the end of one year, there are people who 'swear' that 'it must happen this year.' You are not God, and you are not the Author or Finisher of your faith. It is excellent to make declarations by faith, to call forth things that are not as though they were, and to wage war against demonically orchestrated delays and release answers to prayer about a spouse. After it all, let the peace of God work for you. Let time and the word of God test the strength and purpose of your relationship. Let anything wrong happen before the marriage and see if you will still go ahead. Irrespective of what came against Joseph, he was successful in the end: *Then he sent someone to Egypt ahead of them—Joseph, who was sold as a slave. They bruised his feet with fetters and placed his neck in an iron collar. Until the time came to fulfill his dreams, the Lord tested Joseph's character.*[74]

The duration of testing for each relationship will be different. Abraham's emissary went seeking at the right time and saw a prospective spouse, yet he did not hurry to decide. He took a moment, waited silently, musing, thinking, praying, considering, listening for God's voice of direction: *Then she quickly emptied her pitcher into the trough, ran back to the well to draw water, and drew for all his camels. And the man, wondering at her, remained silent so as to know whether the Lord had made his journey prosperous or not.*[75]

The passage of time and the challenges of life will test the strength of your love and the authenticity of the feelings you have professed for each other; allow them. Let God's timing work for you, not against you. Time will test your character, which is the bedrock of any successful marriage. How you spend your time determines how your life will turn out to be, for your time is your life. If you want to live well and excel in life, you must manage your life's times and seasons.

Time can be lost, wasted, or invested. As my dear husband, John Enelamah says, 'If you keep track of your seconds and days, you will account for your years.' And don't you worry. As Craig Groeschel posted, "If it's not God's time, you cannot force it. If it is God's time, you cannot stop it." Indeed, God holds all the aces, *"But these things I plan won't happen right away. Slowly, steadily, surely, the time approaches when the vision will be fulfilled. If it seems slow, do not despair, for these things will surely come to pass. Just be patient! They will not be overdue a single day!"*[76]

Part II
Marriage Is a Family Affair

God sets the solitary in families.
He brings out those who are bound into prosperity;
But the rebellious dwell in a dry land.[77]

Chapter 6
The principle of equal yokes

The yoke you wear determines the burden you bear

- Edwin Louis Cole

Marriage is a God-agenda as seen in principles that depend heavily on Him - divine activity, prayer, the assignment, and timing. Yet, marriage is also a family agenda. This section explores principles that situate marriage as a family affair and, from our case study, address equal yokes, parental honor, gifts, and service. Marriage as a family affair speaks to your associations and how they affect how you find and keep the love of your life.

Nature and nurture

Think about this: Which came first? The institution of marriage or the family unit that gave rise to the couple? It is like the chicken or the egg question. Do you have to come from a family to enter marriage, or does marriage create a family? It is difficult to say, as both concepts are interconnected. The bottom line is, your marriage will involve others, particularly family. Hardly any marriage can be isolated from family, relatives, or friends. There are always people connected to you one way or the other. Whether you enjoy associating with other people or not, your relationship is going to be affected positively or negatively by your family, your spouse's family, and your other social networks.

Just as you have been born in a particular environment, with your upbringing and history that shaped who you are today, you must understand that your prospective spouse will be shaped by their own unique experiences as well. The environment you were exposed to, particularly during your formative years, your temperament, training, character traits, and habits influence how you interact with others, particularly in your relationship - with your spouse.

Equal yokes

"He (Abraham) said to the senior servant in his household, the one in charge of all that he had, "Put your hand under my thigh. I want you to swear by the LORD, *the God of heaven and the God of earth, that you will not get a wife for my son from the daughters of the Canaanites, among whom I am living, but will go to my country and my own relatives and get a wife for my son Isaac."*[78]

Some questions arise here: was Abraham prejudiced? Where is acceptance of others and love for diversity here? Will returning to his family or relatives to find a wife for Isaac or marry someone known to the family guarantee a successful marriage? Is this a literal demand, or are there underlying meanings attached to this request? What qualities of the Canaanites were less than desirable for Abraham's scion? Why is this so important to this great man?

A sensitive subject

The principle of equal or similar yokes is a sensitive subject, almost bordering on exclusion and selectivity. Sadly, people have interpreted the principle of equal yokes in less than positive ways and used it to advance hatred against others. However, and in truth, you must be selective when it comes to choosing the one you intend to spend the rest of your life with, the one with whom you will live in the same house, perhaps bear children, and the one that will be literally under your skin. Yes, the principle of equal yokes is about selectivity in the choice of a spouse. Look at it this way, as you explore relationships and choose who to do life with, you will come across all kinds of people - some that you connect with or are attracted to. You may even find the one who finds harmony in your life assignments and generally feels good to be around. You can even get to a point where you two have a mutual desire to get married. However, is there congruence on beliefs and how you approach life, especially with the fundamentals such as how you understand or work in the principle of Divine activity.

> *The principle of equal yokes is a sensitive subject, inevitably and almost bordering on exclusion or selectivity in the choice of a spouse.*

Equal yokes are about the spiritual values and beliefs that guide, restrict, or free you to respond in specific ways along life's journey. Choosing your spouse by the principle of equal yokes implies that you must only join with or marry one of your 'kind.' Paul used this term when he admonished the church in Corinth: *Do not be unequally yoked together with unbelievers. For what fellowship has righteousness with lawlessness? And what communion has light with darkness?*[79] When you understand that your choice of a spouse will inadvertently influence your destiny, you must stop to confirm that the prospective one and the yoke about to bind you is similar.

Of Yokes

The subject of 'yokes' was expressly introduced in the law of Moses and forbade hitching two different animals to pull a plow during the farming process: *"You must not plough with an ox and a donkey harnessed together."*[80] In the original sense, unequal yoking suggests that you bound, collared, or coupled two different animals, often unequal in size, together with by a yoke. In a relationship, an unequal yoke is being bound to one with a different spiritual leaning, burden, and inclination as yours.

A yoke is a substantial block of wood placed and tied to the neck of two animals to hold them together and usually attached to a plow, which they pull to till the soil for cultivation. Usually, oxen, donkeys, or horses were yoked to work on fields before the modern-day tractors were invented. With the animals' different stature, traits, and behavioral tendencies, putting a yoke on two different species even if they were of the same height will almost always be counterproductive, not plow effectively, nor get the best results. Even two similar animals with different physical dimensions will require more effort to harness. The goal here is to facilitate the fulfillment of purpose, their assignment.

God formed a wife for Adam different from him, yet of the same kind and comparable to him. Years before Moses received this law from God for the children of Israel, Abraham, their ancestor, had lived by the principle of equal yokes. *'One day Abraham said to his oldest servant, the man in charge of his household, "Take an oath by putting your hand under my thigh. Swear by the Lord, the God of heaven and earth, that you will not allow my son to marry one of these local Canaanite women.*

Go instead to my homeland, to my relatives, and find a wife there for my son Isaac'.[81] When Abraham gave these instructions to his servant, he meant that he did not want Isaac to be unequally yoked. He was neither prejudiced nor biased. It must have been so important that Abraham made his servant swear in such an intimate manner that he will not deviate from his instructions: *"Take an oath by putting your hand under my thigh."*

Abraham did not want Isaac to marry any of the Canaanite girls, nor did he want Isaac to return to the land they had come from to search for a spouse. He recalled what it took him to make the journey out of his homeland in the first place. Terah, Abraham's father, had also embarked on this journey to find a new city. Abraham recalled how his father, Terah, was distracted at Haran after losing his son, Haran; Terah never completed the journey to the Promised Land[82].

> A yoke is a strong block of wood placed and tied on the neck of two animals to hold them together, attached to a plough and pulled to till the soil for cultivation.

Abraham did not want to take chances with Isaac. He remembered that Lot and his family moved to Sodom to live among people who had values significantly opposite to the ones Abraham's lineage lived by - and the outcomes for Lot and his kin.

He, too, had learned some tough lessons when he ventured into a relationship with Hagar to have Ishmael. He had received the hint of destiny and a posterity that would affect all the nations of the world. Even though Abraham would not live to see all that God would do for his generations yet unborn, he could not afford to be careless and miss God's plan for him and his generations yet unborn. Abraham feared God and wanted to please God. Abraham was a man of strong convictions who valued the words God had spoken to Him. He needed to keep Isaac focused on the vision and covenant with God. He wanted to ensure he passed the baton right.

His instruction to his servant was a tall order, just as choosing a spouse will be for you. The condition of ensuring an equal yoke must have seemed incredulous and unmanageable to the servant: *The servant asked, "But what if I can't find a young woman who is willing to travel so far from home? Should I then take Isaac there to live among your relatives in the land you came from?" "No!" Abraham responded. "Be careful never to take my son there. For the LORD, the God of heaven, who took me from my father's house and my native land, solemnly promised to give this land to my descendants. He will send his angel ahead of you, and he will see to it that you find a wife there for my son.*[83]

Attracted, distracted, destructed

Years later, Abraham's grandson, Esau, would become 'unequally yoked' when he married the same women Abraham had not wanted Isaac to wed. Abraham's fears were justified, seeing how Esau's life turned out in the end: *At the age of forty, Esau married two Hittite wives: Judith, the daughter of Beeri, and Basemath, the daughter of Elon. But Esau's wives made life miserable for Isaac and Rebekah.*[84] The Bible does not tell us how Esau's spouses brought sorrow and grief to the parents-in-law (I use spouse and not wives because the non-alignment to the same values and spiritual beliefs could be from the man's or woman's angle). Esau's spouses may have been beautiful women, but something about them did not make for a cordial relationship with Isaac and Rebekah. For you, does it matter that your spouse has a good relationship with your parents?

One wonders why Isaac was liberal about choosing a wife for Esau, given the extent his father went to help him marry right. It could have also been that Esau ignored his parents' 'old school' counsel and instruction. Many years later, the writer of the book of Hebrews had this to say of Esau: ... *See that no one is sexually immoral, or is godless like Esau, who for a single meal sold his inheritance rights as the oldest son.*[85] Could the women Esau married have influenced how he dealt with the various issues in his life or was it vice versa?

Esau was described as sexually immoral; he was either involved in sex before or outside marriage or adultery. He may have struggled with self-control or did not have a heart for God's values. He married three wives,[86] perhaps one woman was not enough, or it was part of ongoing trauma from the fall out of his issues with his brother. It is interesting to observe that the immoral and polygamous culture of the Canaanites that Abraham tried to avoid seemed attractive to Esau and drew him further away from fulfilling his destiny. He quickly despised and sold his birth right to his brother.

Sex orgies were a standard feature in the Canaanite culture, especially during the worship of their gods, and this is contrary to the values of the God of Abraham, who is holy. Similarly, Dinah, Isaac's granddaughter, would associate with the 'daughters of the land,' and one of the young men from that community raped her[87]. Dinah's name no longer mentioned other than in association with this awful incident; she may never have fulfilled her destiny.

King Solomon, the wisest king of all times, would have had a perfect history, but for the relationship choices that marred his 'career' and God's plans for the house of David. His weakness paved the path to the downfall of this sage. He was aware of the consequences of being unequally yoked with the wrong partner and thought he could outsmart the principle by putting everything in its place and in their 'compartments.' His strategy was to keep his 'foreign' wives, who had different values and beliefs, away from God's holy city so that he could still enjoy them without feeling that he was departing from his duties to God.

He knew that it was not suitable for him to have these women since they did not fit into his affiliation with God. He loved them, and obviously loved God much more – the God that had appeared to him, and so blessed him. Perhaps, he hoped that the women would come to believe in his God one day, even if it were for their love for him. Here is what he did: *Solomon moved his wife, Pharaoh's daughter, from the City of David to the new palace he had built for her. He said, "My wife must not live in King David's palace, for the Ark of the* LORD *has been there, and it is holy ground."*[88] He probably thought, 'I have this under control.' He may have even hired teachers or scribes to give special classes to the women about the ways and values of God, hoping they would come around with time - but the assumptions worked against him. Indeed, the choice you make of whom to marry is more important than anything else you will do to make that marriage work[89].

Solomon was unable to draw the line with these women. He was a king of renown, and people traveled from all over the world to hear his

> Solomon thought he could handle the consequences of an unequal yoke by 'putting everything in its place, in compartments'. But the principle worked above his strategy.

wise words and see his style of government. He was a kind of the eighth wonder of the world. Many kings pledged allegiance to him and had all manner of trade and peace treaties with him. Most of the wives he had were king's daughters – perhaps given to him as gifts from the kings who sought to associate with him or was it just the norm then for a king to have so many wives.

Whatever the reason, Solomon accumulated so many wives, generously loved them all, and became a victim of the principle he neglected: *Now King Solomon loved many foreign women. Besides Pharaoh's daughter, he married women from Moab, Ammon, Edom, Sidon, and from among the Hittites. The LORD had clearly instructed the people of Israel, 'You must not marry them, because they will turn your hearts to their gods.'*

He had 700 wives of royal birth and 300 concubines. And in fact, they did turn his heart away from the LORD. In Solomon's old age, they turned his heart to worship other gods instead of being completely faithful to the LORD his God, as his father, David, had been. Solomon worshiped Ashtoreth, the goddess of the Sidonians, and Molech, the detestable god of the Ammonites[90].

The primary reason for the principle of equal yokes, the reason that Abraham did not want Isaac to marry the Canaanite women, was simply this: *that they do not turn his heart away from the Lord*. Dwight D. Eisenhower, in one of his quotes, may have captured the impact of Solomon's choices on his legacy: "*A people that values its privileges above its principles soon loses both.*" Solomon's unequal yokes were in the multiples. He was incredibly wise and erudite yet did not appreciate the power of this principle. Not acting on the knowledge that one has can prove disastrous. That is why a super-intelligent individual who is a high-flier at work may be failing at marriage – because every institution and aspect of life has principles, laws, and skill sets that dictate their success.

What constitutes an equal yoke?

If yokes in a relationship are not literal blocks of wood placed on the neck, what do they represent? First, yokes in relationships are figurative, binding forces and couplings that hold individuals together along a path, hopefully, to accomplish a purpose. Just as yokes join two oxen to plow, a yoke joins a couple to achieve an objective, a marital destiny. Yokes in relationships are like the gear that regulates a car's direction, speed, and state – they are not visible while driving. In finding and choosing the love of your life, the principle of equal yokes has more to do with values, beliefs, and persuasions than material things you share, physical attributes, temperaments, or factors emanating from race or ethnicity. The binding yoke you will have in common with your spouse is primarily the alignment of your heart, your belief (or unbelief) in God or a supreme being. This belief shapes your purpose, values, principles, culture, how you will raise children, acquire, and use resources, manage your gains, joys, pains, losses, and outlook on life overall.

Marriage is the harness on the yoke of a substantial block of sorts binding you two. As a result of the yoke, marriage is often uncomfortable, propelling you in a particular direction with the person you have been yoked with, hopefully wholeheartedly. Because a yoke, by its nature, is heavy, it is like a burden (that you hopefully love to bear), but that will sometimes feel painful and restrictive. Even for the animals plowing under a yoke, there are certainly times when one would prefer to sit and chew the cord, while the other would have sighted a pile of hay at the other side and would want to go off in that direction. However, the yoke binding them prevents either of them from going in the direction they prefer and constrains them in the direction their yoke-partner wants them to go or where they agree to go. When there is a consistent difference in the direction either of the two would like to go, a skirmish however gentle or violent ensues, and stress builds up.

If you decide to travel the road of life fastened to another, in this case, a spouse, then it should be with someone that you have good reason to be in this constraint with, someone you agree with. Amos asked: *'Can two people walk together without agreeing on the direction?'*

An unequal yoke and the tension it will bring to a relationship is a distraction to fulfilling your purpose and destiny and may ultimately bring you much pain and sorrow. God's instruction to the children of Israel not to marry other nations that worshiped idols was clear. *You must not intermarry with them. Do not let your daughters and sons marry their sons and daughters, for they will lead your children away from me to worship other gods. Then the anger of the Lord will burn against you, and he will quickly destroy you.*[91]

> Figuratively, yokes are binding forces, and they hold individuals together along a path, hopefully to accomplish a purpose.

Right in Isaac's family and in Esau's life, the influence of the daughters of the land had come to stay. Rebekah saw the impact and outcome of marriage with women of unequal yokes on Esau and hinged her decision to send Jacob away to her brother on that. She wanted to ensure that Jacob would not tow the same line as Esau and add more grief and sorrow to their broken hearts. Isaac gave Jacob, his son, a similar instruction like his father had given several years ago: *So, Isaac called for Jacob, blessed him, and said, "You must not marry any of these Canaanite women. Instead, go at once to Paddan-aram, to the house of your grandfather Bethuel, and marry one of your uncle Laban's daughters*[92]. Isaac could attest to the values that Laban stood for. He could not afford for things to go wrong a second time. All the efforts by Abraham, his father to preserve his posterity for God would have been futile. Even though it seemed like Jacob was running from the consequences of deceiving Esau his brother, going to Paddan-aram was an opportunity for him to find an equal yoke in marriage and ultimately preserve the promise to Abraham.

The principle of equal yokes is much more overarching than opposites or personality differences. Even though opposing magnetic fields attract, an unequal yoke in marriage is more than that, it is a recipe for disaster.

Ruth and Paul

Ruth and Paul had met on Facebook. Ruth was a first-grade teacher, and Paul was an accountant. Ruth had grown up in a family where their parents always emphasized their faith and relationship with God. When she met Paul, and they began to grow close, she was concerned that Paul was not a professing Christian, though he said he loved God and was exploring the faith. Paul still struggled with drinking and watching pornography, but Ruth continued to pray earnestly for him.

Within a year, Ruth and Paul would get married. Soon after they had their son, their conflicts began. There were frequent fights and arguments over minor things. It seemed like they disagreed on almost everything. Paul refused to pray with her each evening as they had initially agreed and stayed out extremely late with friends at the pub.

Ruth was too ashamed to share her marriage woes with her parents and friends as things grew worse. Months later, Ruth would wake up to a handwritten note Paul had left at her bedside. Paul had filed for a divorce where he complained that Ruth was too religious and trying to manipulate him into becoming a fanatic. What? She could not believe this was happening. Paul had never committed to the faith, and Ruth was gullible, as she believed every word he had said. Ruth had met Paul, a nice guy that goes to church, says all the right words, and behaves appropriately. However, it appeared that Paul may have been in transition in his low moment, just trying out church and did not share the same values as she did. Ruth and Paul were unequally yoked; she had ignored the red flags or probably was too blinded by the excitement of having someone who expressed love and leaned on her, or perhaps, she might have been desperate to get married.

The most desirable yoke

Even though yokes may seem uncomfortable, there is one that is easy to bear, a yoke required to be successful in every aspect of life. This is the yoke that Abraham was promised, and later Moses would speak to the children of Israel about. Jesus said, *"Come to me, all of you who are weary and carry heavy burdens, and I will give you rest. Take my yoke upon you. Let me teach you because I am humble and gentle at heart, and you will find rest for your souls. For my yoke is easy to bear, and the burden I give you is light."*[93]

> Even though yokes may seem uncomfortable, there is a yoke that is easy to bear, which is required to be successful in every aspect of life.

Jesus offers this yoke that you must seek with your spouse, the yoke of the heart - your beliefs, your spiritual source, and your faith. The writer of Proverbs said, *"Above all else, guard your heart, for everything you do flows from it."*[94] Another translation put it this way: *Guard your heart above all else, for it determines the course of your life*. I like the continued use of the word – 'guard,' an action word that is translated as to stand sentinel, like a soldier or to watch over to protect or control - your heart. The heart is the primary yoke "matter" in relationships, the neck upon which the block of wood (the precepts, the principles of God, and life) are written. When there is an alignment of belief and faith, these beliefs or values will inevitably determine the course of your life. When Solomon and Esau left their hearts unguarded, the contrary seed of their love interests was planted in their hearts, and the fruit was inevitable.

To walk in the principle of yokes

To prepare to walk in the principle of equal yokes, you must examine yourself. Before marriage, you want to ensure that the other's beliefs, values, or life philosophies align with yours. People often say that you cannot know anyone sufficiently to understand their values; however, people always speak through their words, actions, and fruit to anyone who cares to listen.

Primarily, the principle of equal yokes expects a believer to marry a fellow believer with whom they agree on the most fundamental aspects of their faith. *Do not be yoked together with unbelievers. For what do righteousness and wickedness have in common? Or what fellowship can light have with darkness?*[95] For those who profess to follow God, His instruction is explicit about a believer's relationship with an unbeliever. In addition, there are different frames and levels of belief. If you are a person of faith and not yoked to another who confesses Christ as Lord and Savior, you have inadvertently become yoked to one who is bound to another, and as simple as it seems, it is crucial to identify and name that 'other.'

The primary basis for latching on to a significant other should be that you agree in your connection to the Divine. What does your desired or prospective spouse believe in? What you hold dear, and the way you believe will drive your actions and your responses to the different situations that life will surely throw your way.

A word of caution

Many will pretend to be who they are not and convince themselves that they are who they are not. Some people are confused about their beliefs and hope a relationship will help clarify them. A discerning heart and the unity of all the principles working together will help you. It is advisable not to wait until it is too late to realize the consequences of unequal yokes in marriage. Paul wrote: *Don't you realize that your bodies are parts of*

To prevent your attraction to someone of a different race or culture from being an unequal yoke, both parties must make the commitment to understand and respect each other's background, differences and decide how to manage relationships and expectations from family and other affiliations

---

Christ? Should a man take his body, which is part of Christ, and join it to a prostitute? Never! And don't you realize that if a man joins himself t a prostitute, he becomes one body with her? For the Scriptures say, "The two are united into one."[96] Unless like Hosea, you were asked to go and get married to a prostitute for a purpose - to illustrate God's unconditional love and restoration to Israel, be sure to take Paul's words to heart.

Is ethnicity or race a factor in unequal yokes?

I teach a course on the implications of race and culture, and this topic is as tense as can be. Yet, I will delve in a little because of the dichotomy I have observed, re ethnicity and yokes. You can experience a pseudo unequal yoke (in behavioral terms) when you get married to someone from different ethnicity and ignore how your cultural differences (even in Christian culture and even within your ethnicity) could affect your relationship. To manage these differences, it would be good to reflect on what has shaped you to become who you are, discuss your expectations, and acknowledge the differences that might bring a potential conflict. If you or your prospective one come from different ethnicities, you must be aware of and be proactive in managing any differences related to your relationship. That said, we are equal before God, and there is no discrimination in Christ.

When you get married, one thing is sure; you begin to either grow together or drift apart. For those called to marry, a successful marriage is an important vehicle to help you achieve your purpose in life. An unequal yoke will constitute a thorn in the flesh in the course of your destiny, but that will not be your story. In summary, equal yokes speak of an agreement in faith, purpose, values, and beliefs. When the storms of life begin to batter on the boat of your marriage, the common yoke of your faith in Christ which you both have agreed to bear under will keep you steady until you make it to the other side.

In the words of Bishop Bronner, "before you get married, discuss bills, parenting styles, credit, debt, religion, how to deal with family, what beliefs will be instilled in your children, childhood traumas, sexual expectations, partner expectations, financial expectations, family health history, mental health history, bucket list, dream home, careers and education, political views and whatever else comes to mind – love alone is not enough." It could not have been said better.

This is the process of both understanding and weighing the equality of the yokes you are choosing to bear, with spirituality as number one issue to clarify, and facilitators of parental honor that we will examine in the next chapter.

Chapter 7
The principle of parental honor

We never know the love of a parent till we become parents ourselves.

– Henry Ward Beecher

Graham and Anita were engaged and looked forward to getting married. When Graham proposed over Christmas, Anita's parents tried to discourage her from going ahead with the relationship. They did not think Graham was the right person for their daughter. Anita was adamant because her parents could not give a specific reason for their opinion. She held onto Graham and would not let go even though her parents were uncomfortable with their relationship. Graham appeared to be in a hurry to be married and threatened to move on with another woman whose family would take him for who he is if Anita was no longer interested. That made Anita desperate. They had a secret wedding with only a few friends in attendance.

Anita's dad was indifferent, but her mum was distraught. Within a year of getting married, a different side of Graham emerged. He would not return home several nights in a row, and when Anita would question him, he would ask her to go back to her parents if she could. Anita had a severe bout of depression; she was stuck with a person who would not allow her to go anywhere but did everything he wanted. Anita was not allowed to work; she could not visit her family, and they could not visit either, yet Graham was not there for her. Anita was shocked when she found out very dark secrets about Graham's lifestyle and childhood, including abuse.

Many would think it overbearing that parents' opinion should matter or have any bearing in choosing a life partner. But the patriarch, Abraham, was not going to leave anything to chance. Abraham must have had those discussions with Isaac and his mother, and they hoped that God would direct them through the process when the time came. Abraham's oldest servant had been there through his master's life journeys. He had watched Abraham seek God's face as he waited for the promised child. The servant saw Isaac grow up before his very eyes, knew him well, and now, he has been entrusted to facilitate the process that would birth the next generation of his master's pedigree. He understood and imbibed his master's belief system and values.

Even though Abraham appeared to have commissioned the search for a wife, it was still up to Isaac to make the final choice when he saw Rebekah. Abraham was not the one who went to receive the wife, and he was no longer mentioned in the relationship between Isaac and his wife. Yet, Isaac trusted his father and servant to support the process; they were his community, his people. He also spent time waiting, meditating, and praying that God would direct the servant to the woman who would be exactly right for him. Someone once said that it takes a village to raise a child. Isaac's community that had been around him had watched him grow.

"No man is an island"

No matter how much you think you are walking the life path alone or are 'self-made,' you are not alone. Perhaps you were abandoned, orphaned, or without any close parental links; there are always a host of individuals surrounding your life that have affected your growth and development (hopefully for good). Starting from the one who carried you in the womb and gave birth to you, irrespective of their role in your life, even if they did not raise you, they are a part of you. The events that occurred before and during the nine months you were in the womb affect outcomes in your life. There is much research and debate about nature, nurture, and epigenetics, which I cannot take on here. Yet, you are more connected to your kin, known or unknown, than you can reckon.

> You are connected to your kin, known or unknown, more than you reckon

God can and will use your parents, guardians, or significant others in your life to influence your choice of a spouse. These people see sides of you that you cannot see by yourself. The principle of parental honor or approval refers to the consent - spoken or unspoken, sought for or not - given by parents, guardians, or those who have played a part in your growth and development or who have been a strong influence in your life. When parents are no longer alive, separated, or you never lived with them, you still find yourself weighing your decision against the opinion of that visible or invisible figure. After you leave home or start living independently, most parents are still positioned to provide spiritual guidance in choosing a spouse.

The principle of parental honor expects that you seek the opinion, approval, acceptance, permission, and blessing of godly parents or guardians (where living) in your choice of a spouse, no matter how sure you are, before you commit to getting married. Approval may sound like a strong word in this age of 'it's my life, and I can do/get what I want,' but to err on the side of sounding archaic, I will retain the word approval. In some cases, you are living far away from home, meet someone that sparks your interest, fall in love, a relationship ensues, and you decide on the spur of the moment to go ahead to get married. The principle of parental honor requires that you at least sound out or share a hint to the parental figures in your life before you make such a monumental decision. That should not take away the intuitiveness or spontaneity of when to pop the question. Usually, you would have been considering the individual before you came to that point of decision.

You could also be a very self-reliant person who has learned to depend on your intuition for decision-making and has developed the practice of listening to your heart's quiet voice. In that case, it is possible to tell if you have met the one and may not desire to seek the counsel, but only inform a parental figure or guardian. Often, more intuitive ladies would have sensed or imagined earlier than men that they have met the one and perhaps hinted or discussed this relationship with significant friends or mentors in their life. You can know over time or on the spur of the moment that 'this is the one.' However, there is no harm in taking a step back to sound out your parents or guardians about your plans and listen for comments or questions that may be pointers weighing your options. If you are someone who favors informed decisions or if you have grown to hear and understand how God leads you in life, there is a chance that your conviction may be stronger than any parental figure's opinion.

> *The parental honor principle is a general term that includes (where applicable) a consideration of the counsel of parents, guardians, mentors, or true spiritual overseers who play a significant role in your life or who your look up to...*

Recognize that opinion is different from consent. More so, it is not necessarily for them to agree with or disapprove of your choice – it is more about the honor of the principle.

Is there a middle ground?

Overall, it is essential to have some level of agreement with unbiased (hard one) parents, guardians, mentors, or spiritual overseers in your life to choose who you are planning to marry. While you are not looking to anyone to be 100% on the same page with you (after all, they are not the ones going into the union), godly counsel or sincere critiques on your choice (hopefully on things you can work on) is necessary. The principle of parental honor aims for you to benefit from the wisdom of parents in issues you are blind to, which you may need to address before you tie the knot. Most likely, your parents or guardians have been part of your life in one way or another. I hope that they are wise and have a record of sound judgment. I hope they know a lot about you, especially what is hidden from you but known to others. I hope that they are unafraid and able to tell you the truth in love.

If the foundations are right, godly parental overseers could provide counsel, and influence your choice. But if the foundations are faulty or destroyed, what can you do? There are situations where parents would not approve of God's choice of a spouse for their children for no good reason - culture, race, or socioeconomic status.

Sometimes dissenting parents remain adamant over a long period. We had heard of parents who sued a church for conducting a wedding for their child when the parents did not consent. It is crucial to get a sense of where parents are regarding the relationship or prospective one, and better still hear their heart and prayer for the relationship. At times, the refusal to give their consent or approve of their child's choice could be for a season or short period and may be unpleasant. However, if you have prayed and are convinced that this individual is the right one for you, the period of waiting for your parents to come around to it or to see 'what you are seeing' and that you have made the right choice is an opportunity for growth as you work on other aspects of the relationship pending when they change their minds. Periods of waiting for parental approval may also serve as a 'fire' that will test the integrity of the relationship. All things being equal, parental consent should serve as a confirmation of your choice of a spouse.

Parental disapproval is a solid reason to delay your wedding plans, at least for a while. Let the passage of time confirm your choice as you wait upon God for the future of your relationship. Even though some parents or guardians may not know all the details of your life, they still do know something you may not know about yourself. They may be concerned about specific repeated patterns, health susceptibilities, or mistakes in your life like theirs and have insight that should prevent history from repeating itself.

A mum who watched you grow or, even if you did not live with her, may see traits you exhibit that may or may not have characterized their life or her parent's lives that she had not discussed with you. Wisdom demands that you will be sensitive and discerning to at the least, listen to the observations and opinions of your parents and sincerely weigh them to see how this influences your choice of a spouse positively or negatively. If there are negative issues that could affect your relationship, you can then wage your war to address these or break curses, where they are in operation, and chart a new destiny with knowledge and wisdom. That is essentially what organizations do in strategic planning, they refuse to operate blindly.

The parents, Abraham and Laban were involved in their children's marital process. Both parents essentially consented without meeting the prospective individuals on either side. This may be good or bad depending on the context. So, it was not about the son of the emissary's master being rich and handsome, nor did Abraham's instruction include how beautiful the woman would be. Rebekah's family was astonished at the serendipity of how the servant was directed in his quest. They asked Rebekah what she thought – they were not choosing for her but merely stewarding the process. They asked if she was willing to commit to getting married to Isaac. They had listened to the servant's narrative; they knew the values his master, Abraham, held dear, and the kind of family their daughter would be joining.

In some ethnic groups, like my Igbo, parents would send an inquirer, '*onye ajuju*' who may evolve into a marriage witness, '*onye aka ebe*' to go find out about the family and their background before a final decision or concessions are made on giving away their daughter and vice versa. It is like the due diligence and CORI background check organizations carry out before hiring; how much more families should do for this more significant relationship. You are willing to follow a process and offer personal information to get hired for a job that is often short-term – why should you think it such a big deal that families should make some inquiries about the one you would spend the rest of your life with? Of course, people present an 'I am in love' argument, and there are always deviations from the mean in life.

> 'Parental' honor and approval is one of the tools that God will use to help you choose your spouse

Both Rebekah and Isaac's families, in this case, approved this union and acknowledged that divine activity was at play: *Then Laban and Bethuel replied, "The* LORD *has obviously brought you here, so there is nothing we can say. Here is Rebekah; take her and go. Yes, let her be the wife of your master's son, as the* LORD *has directed."*[97] They approved the servant's proposal. Although everything happened quickly, it did not feel like a rushed or difficult choice and decision to make. There was no record of a warning check or unease in their hearts that this could be the wrong decision. For instance, there is the record of Dinah's brothers expressing their concern that Shechem would not be an ideal spouse for their sister, given his antecedents. Samson's parents also questioned his choice of a spouse.

And though Rebekah's family accepted the servant's proposal, it was she who made the choice to get married to Isaac: *"Well,"* they said, *"we'll call Rebekah and ask her what she thinks." So, they called Rebekah. "Are you willing to go with this man?" they asked her. And she replied, "Yes, I will go."*[98] It was a proposal and acceptance by proxy, and it still happens today.

Marriage is a family affair

Abraham was not only interested in a spouse for Isaac, his son, but he also prayed and instructed his servant about the kind of family he should search for a wife: *...swear by the Lord, the God of heaven and the God of the earth, that you will not take a wife for my son from the daughters of the Canaanites, among whom I dwell; but you shall go to my country and to my family, and take a wife for my son Isaac."* [99] Rebekah's family was not complacent either; they were actively involved in the process.

Laban, Rebekah's brother, knew of Abraham, and though they listened to the servant's testimony of his master, if they were unsure about going ahead with a commitment, they would have expressed it.

Abraham's servant sought their consent: *"Then I bowed low and worshiped the Lord. I praised the Lord, the God of my master, Abraham, because he had led me straight to my master's niece to be his son's wife. So, tell me—will you or won't you show unfailing love and faithfulness to my master? Please tell me yes or no, and then I'll know what to do next." Then Laban and Bethuel replied, "The Lord has obviously brought you here, so there is nothing we can say. Here is Rebekah; take her and go. Yes, let her be the wife of your master's son, as the Lord has directed."*[100]

Her family approved, gave their consent, and confirmed the perception of the servant. Even though the Bible is silent about any reservations that Abraham's servant or Rebekah's family might have had, one can only imagine there would be none. Issues like moving so far away to another country, no longer taking on her roles in the family, and concerns about whether the marriage will work must have been on their mind. They even asked for more time with her, perhaps to express their concerns, come to terms with the new development, the impending journey, or arrive at a closure concerning her destiny.

The principle of parental honor is significant because when a couple gets married, their families become kin, with the couple joining to begin a new family unit. Everyone brings their physical, spiritual, and emotional heritage to the new family line, and whatever stock they are of influences the marriage positively or negatively. Some families or parents may have made spiritual commitments or entered covenants that altered the destiny of their children. So, it is always good to know what you are signing up for.

The background of the spouse you marry affects the quality of your marriage and may influence the fulfillment of your destiny. Abraham had a unique and life-changing encounter with the God of the whole earth. God made promises to Abraham about his descendants, and this redefined his destiny. Abraham's part in the choice of Isaac's wife was a way of passing on the baton to ensure that the race is completed, and in essence, God's promises would stand a better chance of being fulfilled. What purpose would you and your prospective partner advance?

In the same way that blessings are transferred from one generation to the next, curses or behavioral patterns are also conveyed, unless there is a conscious effort or divine intervention to break the chain effect. You do not have to endure or live with the burden of negative patterns, curses, or situations that translate over generations of your family — you can and should ask God to change your destiny. Just as Abraham entered a covenant with God and re-wrote his destiny, you can enter a covenant with God to live a life that will please Him, and He will make all things new, enabling you to live a fulfilled and abundant life: *Therefore, if anyone is in Christ, he is a new creation; old things have passed away; behold, all things have become new*[101].

Your family background, upbringing, culture, exposures, and experiences in life will play a part in defining who you become in life. Even though your prospective spouse is attractive, and you both enjoy each other's company, you should consider how you will both blend and create your new lifestyle as a family and ensure that you talk about it with each other. The goal here is to appreciate where you are both coming from, your differences, and devise your winning strategy for a relationship enriched by the best of both your families. Often, people do not realize how much their past has shaped them as they enter a relationship. You are getting married to your spouse, but you both will not be isolated and would have to relate with each other's family.

Listening with your heart

You benefit from a different perspective of life when you consider the counsel from godly parents or guardians. Many intending couples tend to overlook crucial issues when they plan to marry. The excitement of new or puppy love is often blinding and full of irrational decisions. Many times, young couples decide to get married because they cannot keep their hands off each other even when they know they are not quite right for each other in other ways. Physical attraction is not sufficient to sustain a marriage in the long run. Consider the actual amount of time spent together in bed in comparison to the time allotted to other aspects of life.

Often, it is difficult to face the truth about certain things you observe about a person that you admire and want to be in a relationship with. Sometimes, only family or parents are bold enough to tell you the truth to your face about their observations and the reality of your relationship. An open mind will choose to hear at the very least, and then make your decisions with foresight.

> *The principle of parental honor hangs on a promise and offers a covering as you honor your parents or guardian's counsel*

When your parents or guardian have any reservations, the wise thing to do is to listen to their concerns even if it is painful at the time or might disrupt your wedding plans or goals. Find time to talk to God about it -remember the principle of Divine activity; if He designed you for marriage, He would indeed have something to say about your choice and plans. It is often easier said (to break off that relationship) than done because of the realities on the ground, social pressure, or the people who know you were in a relationship and planning to wed. But I can assure you that a broken engagement or relationship is always better than a broken marriage.

Samson and Delilah are famous/infamous for their relationship. Samson's parents were concerned about the women he was attracted to, who ultimately led him away from his purpose and to his downfall. He had so much potential but did not have a great ending despite it all. To his credit, he at least knew to sound his parents out on his intentions: *One day when Samson was in Timnah, one of the Philistine women caught his eye. When he returned home, he told his father and mother, "A young Philistine woman in Timnah caught my eye. I want to marry her. Get her for me." His father and mother objected. "Isn't there even one woman in our tribe or among all the Israelites you could marry?" they asked. "Why must you go to the <u>pagan</u> Philistines to find a wife?" But Samson told his father, "Get her for me! She looks good to me."*[102]

Samson's parents disapproved of the women he found appealing. Have you ever thought about what you find appealing, what catches your eye? His parents felt that his choice of relationships with these women constituted an unequal yoke for him, as they were nonbelievers in God. Samson went ahead regardless. Unknown to his parents, God allowed Samson to marry the wrong person so that He could deliver Israel from the oppression of the Philistines. If you want to go ahead to break the principle of equal yokes and parental honor as Samson did, please confirm that the Lord is directing you to do so – for a purpose. With Samson, here was a case of the principle of divine activity overriding or superseding the principle of equal yokes and parental honor, and we will talk more about this in the overriding principle of God's will for your life. A similar situation occurred when God asked Hosea to get into an unequal yoke by marrying a spouse who was a prostitute. God wanted to use this union to illustrate His unconditional love for His children.

Some young couples go ahead with their plans to get married with or without their parent's honor or approval. Sometimes these choices seem so ideal and so innocent, with no imminent dangers or known unequal yoke issues. However, it is always important to listen to the still small voice, as there might be issues to contend with in the marriage long after the wedding is over.

Bringing it together, so far, an understanding of God's sovereignty, the power of prayer, understanding your assignment, the times and seasons of your life, and the importance of being equally yoked will enable you to value the importance of parental honor. In a normal situation, parents invest time and resources from childhood to adulthood to see that children develop and function in society. It is always interesting that when these same children grow older, these parents' views are no longer considered relevant. Parents and guardians are not just there to train, provide, or be inherited from; it is respectful to involve them in this critical decision of your life.

In recent times, parents' opinions, consent, and wisdom have been largely ignored and undermined by young people who feel they know what they want and what is right for them. Although in some instances, the couple feels justified and may choose to ignore the counsel from their parents, especially when these parents have not been the best of examples or shown good judgment in other situations.

The principle with a promise

Seeking parental approval or carrying your parents along as you seek to find and choose the one is a way to honor and treat them with respect, in keeping with the Ten Commandments. The principle of parental honor comes with a promise: *"Honor your father and mother. Then you will live a long, full life in the land the Lord your God is giving you."*[103] Paul also writes, *Children, obey your parents because you belong to the Lord, for this is the right thing to do.* "Honor your father and mother." This is the *first commandment with a promise: If you honor your father and mother, "things will go well for you, and you will have a long life on the earth."*[104]

Seeking and considering the views and approval of your godly parents as you seek to find the love of your life honors them. God can use your parents, even those who do not know or fear Him, to confirm His will for you. The hearts of parents and guardians, who are like the kings and overseers of your life, are in God's hands, and He can use them to guide you, especially if they have the track record of raising you to become the successful and wise person that you are today (reading this book…): *The king's heart is like a stream of water directed by the Lord; he guides it wherever he pleases.*[105]

Chapter 8
The principle of gifts

The gift of a person will open doors for him, and before the great, it gives him access.[106]

-King Solomon

Brenda admired Ben so much while they were in college. Ben was great with the guitar and was

You give three kinds of gifts - your time, treasure, and talent.

famous for organizing gigs in and around town. He was a local star of sorts. She did not stop to think of it when Ben began to take notice of her and they started dating. Brenda and Ben were on the verge of planning to get married when Brenda wondered why she wanted to spend the rest of her life with him. She did not quite love Ben; she was attracted to his gift and fame, his popularity, and all the attention she got as they traveled around. Barely one year after they left college, they went their separate ways, the relationship fizzled out and they never got married.

The principle of the gifts and *giftings* (personal endowments) that you give or receive, like the principle of prayer, paves the way for better results from your efforts. Abraham and his team were wise. With faith and an assurance that the mission would be successful, the servant traveled prepared, armed with gifts for the prospective bride: *The servant watched her in silence, wondering whether or not the Lord had given him success in his mission. Then at last, when the camels had finished drinking, he took out a gold ring for her nose and two large gold bracelets for her wrists.*[107] He gave generously. Just as prayers and praises ascend as a pleasing sacrifice and sweet-smelling incense to God, gifts stir up a response from both God and man.

A gift could be material, an endowment, a service, or talent that an individual possesses and releases to another. Until it is given, it is not a gift. A gift opens doors and often gets you the attention you desire. The wise man wrote: *A gift opens the way and ushers the giver into the presence of the great*[108]. No matter how wealthy or influential a person may be, most people love to receive gifts now and then. Gifts are pleasant, and if one of your love languages is receiving gifts, you may be inclined to relationships with people who give liberally. Gifts are precious. Giving gifts could make your friends pleasantly disposed towards you. The exchange of gifts helps to build warm and cordial relationships. Givers usually have many friends.

Abraham's servant employed the principle of gifts in his search for a wife for Isaac. It was not only to Rebekah that he gave gifts but also to her family Laban, Rebekah's brother must have been impressed by the gifts brought by Abraham's servant. It was not difficult for Laban to welcome Abraham's servant into their home when he saw the gifts, even if he would disagree with the servant's mission. The gifts got the servant a leg in the door: *Now Rebekah had a brother named Laban, who ran out to meet the man at the spring. He had seen the nose-ring and the bracelets on his sister's wrists and had heard Rebekah tell what the man had said.*

So he rushed out to the spring, where the man was still standing beside his camels. Laban said to him, "Come and stay with us, you who are blessed by the Lord! Why are you standing here outside the town when I have a room all ready for you and a place prepared for the camels?"[109] Even if the gifts were not going to sway Laban's opinion on the issue, they at least got his attention and made him stop to consider the case at hand and invite the man home.

The gifts reflected the graciousness, liberality, and commitment to the mission by Abraham and Isaac. The generous gifts were saying to Rebekah and her family that she could expect to be well taken care of and not be in penury by getting married to Isaac. As the discussion with Rebekah's family went on, the servant gave more: *When Abraham's servant heard their answer, he bowed down to the ground and worshiped the Lord. Then he brought out silver and gold jewelry and clothing and presented them to Rebekah. He also gave expensive presents to her brother and mother.*[110] Life and indeed relationships are about giving and receiving.

A gift influences your decisions

There are accounts of gifts that were given with the wrong motives as bribes. As evil as the intentions of bribes are, they illustrate the power of gifts to achieve a desired, often biased result: *A bribe (gift) is seen as a charm by the one who gives it; they think success will come at every turn.*[111] Gifts with ignoble intentions are bribes. Moses warned against the use of gifts to influence any decision. *...Never accept a bribe (gift, bait, or carrot), for they blind the eyes of the wise and corrupt the decisions of the godly.*[112] In this way, the principle of gifts can be abused as one seeks to find the love of their life. While a gift may open a door, it could corrupt and distort your judgment. However, the principle of gifts has its place and works best when all the other principles are in alignment, and the individuals are operating from pure hearts.

Gifts in relationships go on errands and have motives, preferably unselfish ones. Abraham's servant gave gifts to appreciate the lovely woman who took the time to serve him and his entourage. He gave gifts to appreciate the family that took him in for the night. He gave gifts in gratitude to the Lord that had led him thus far. He gave gifts for ordered steps, since he being in the way, was led to Abraham's relatives. He gave gifts in response to their approval and consent for their daughter to marry his master's son. You can always find a reason to give gifts and be thankful in life. His gifts reflected the value he had placed on Rebekah. Of course, no gift could put a price on Rebekah, but a gift is still a gift.

> It takes thoughtfulness to give. It may never occur to you that you are meeting a need because people dress up their troubles all the time. It is better to err on the side of giving rather than assume that the receiver is well resourced.

Expense vs sacrifice

When you have identified a prospective individual, you may not have so much to give in terms of gold and expensive material as Abraham's servant did — what is essential is the desire and a willing heart. God looks at our hearts. In the area of giving, Paul writes that God judges according to what we have and not what is lacking: *For if the willingness is there, the gift is acceptable according to what one has, not according to what one does not have.*[113] Jesus said that the widow who gave her two coins gave more than those who gave out their lavish wealth[114]. So, it is not about the quantity, but more like the difference between equality and equity.

The principle of the gift is not so much about giving expensive things but the thought and sincerity of heart, and the sacrifice. Giving is a result of the condition of the heart. If you are not a generous person (male or female), even while seeking a relationship and the prospective person or their family agrees with your idea, it may never cross your mind to present a gift or try to be a blessing. You can even justify it to yourself that they already have more than enough and do not need your gift. A heart of gratitude and its expression through giving is a character trait, habit, and value you must strive to acquire.

What gifts can be given?

You can give three kinds of gifts including your time, treasure, and talent. There is a cultural expectation that the man will be the one to give and keep giving but giving goes both ways. Recall that Rebekah, the woman, was the first to give of her resource in this case. She used her craft to draw water from the well. She used her strength and energy and invested her time to give water to the servant, his entourage, and their camels. Gifts operate from both sides of the equation — the man or the woman.

Your words of encouragement, kindness, and prayers for the prospective one or their family are invaluable gifts. Nothing is too small or too trivial. Here is an example: Ruth had gone to work,

> Rebekah, the woman, was the first to give. She gave of her resource (using her utensil to draw water from the well), of her strength, energy, and of her time.

and the business owner happened to be doing the rounds on that day and noticed her. He readily gave her a gift. *"Listen, my daughter. Stay right here with us when you gather grain; don't go to any other fields. Stay right behind the young women working in my field. See which part of the field they are harvesting, and then follow them. I have warned the young men not to treat you roughly. And when you are thirsty, help yourself to the water they have drawn from the well." Ruth fell at his feet and thanked him warmly. "What have I done to deserve such kindness?" she asked. "I am only a foreigner."*

"Yes, I know," Boaz replied. "But I also know about everything you have done for your mother-in-law since the death of your husband. I have heard how you left your father and mother and your own land to live here among strangers. May the Lord, the God of Israel, under whose wings you have come to take refuge, reward you fully for what you have done." "I hope I continue to please you, sir," she replied. "You have comforted me by speaking so kindly to me, even though I am not one of your workers."[115]

The initial gifts from Boaz to Ruth were words of affirmation, kindness, and encouragement. Who knew how she was feeling that day? Maybe she felt discouraged and weary trying to make ends meet, and wondered if she made the right decision by returning to Israel with her mother-in-law? Through his words, Boaz encouraged her. He gave her the gifts of counsel, access, and the opportunity to move up. Boaz acknowledged her efforts and offered her security and a conducive environment to work. That day, he promoted her from a part-time to full-time worker with benefits, if she so desired.

His next gift was a meal. At mealtime, Boaz said to her, *"Come over here. Have some bread and dip it in the wine vinegar." "When she sat down with the harvesters, he offered her some roasted grain. She ate all she wanted and had some left over."*[116] Even in cultures where women prefer to pick up the bill, I have yet to find anyone who does not appreciate receiving a gift now and then.

Boaz also gave Ruth another indirect gift. Boaz told his servants to purposely help make her work easier and more manageable and leave behind grains for her to pick and add to whatever she had gleaned at the end of the day. She might not have known that the bounty she took home that period was not from her effort alone. *As she got up to glean, Boaz gave orders to his men, "Let her gather among the sheaves and don't reprimand her. Even pull out some stalks for her from the bundles and leave them for her to pick up, and don't rebuke her."*[117]

Ruth's life began to change when she met Boaz. There was no established relationship between these two and no ulterior motives attached to the giving. Ruth went home with so much to share with Naomi. She must have been so encouraged by that encounter and the generosity. This reminds me of the scripture that says that *"the man (one) who finds a wife (spouse) finds a treasure, and he receives favor from the Lord."*[118] One of the signs of finding the right one is increased levels of unmerited favor. Is your relationship sapping your joy and energy, or is it bringing favor your way? The gift of the other in your life, in the right relationship, should leave you feeling elevated and not deflated. The right relationship even in the lack of resources does not leave you empty-hearted or empty-handed.

Later, when Boaz considered getting married to Ruth, he would give gifts to Ruth's mother-in-law, Naomi: *He also said, "Bring me the shawl you are wearing and hold it out." When she did so, he poured into it six measures of barley and placed the bundle on her. Then he went back to town. When Ruth came to her mother-in-law, Naomi asked, "How did it go, my daughter?" Then she told her everything Boaz had done for her and added, "He gave me these six measures of barley, saying, 'Don't go back to your mother-in-law empty-handed.'"*[119] It was a ripple effect.

> It takes thoughtfulness to give. It may never occur to you that you are meeting a need because people dress their troubles up most of the time. Give anyway.

Thoughtfulness, giving and extended relationships

Just like Abraham's servant, Boaz gave liberally. He was not stingy or frivolous, he was thoughtful in his giving. It takes thoughtfulness to give.

Ruth and Naomi were going through a rough patch. It may never occur to you that when you give, you are meeting a need because people dress their troubles up most of the time. When people look like they have everything they need, give anyway. It is better to err on the side of giving rather than assume that the receiver is well resourced and does not need your gift. In addition, it is commonly said that givers never lack. Therefore, the principle of giving adds value to both the giver and the receiver. Even though you may feel that you do not have much to offer, you have enough. In life, strive to live in abundance, be a generous giver, and be a blessing to others.

In some contexts, families enjoy the camaraderie of giving and receiving gifts from marriage relationships. In those settings, anyone who is not a generous person but seeks a relationship from that family has indirectly identified themselves as a closed conduit and poor candidate for consideration. It is assumed that a marriage will be a blessing to others, particularly the extended family. Sometimes a family observes a prospective spouse and figures this one is not a giver. They will say "this one will cut us off from our child," and begin to suggest to their child that the individual will not make a good spouse. It is often unspoken, but the issue of how resources will flow (or not) in a relationship is a significant consideration in the choice of a spouse.

Today, many married couples are at war with themselves and their extended family in situations where the give and take relationship is botched. This is especially the case in cultures like mine where parents consider their children as their investment – they had spent their all and made many sacrifices to train their child, expecting that when the child is established, the child will, in turn, take care

> *Just as Christ gave himself for the Church, couples in a relationship or desiring to enter one need to cultivate that heart of a giver.*

Principles from the Greatest Family Marriage Dynasty

of them in their old age, similar to a retirement plan. This viewpoint is especially true in contexts where there is no social protection from the government. Sometimes, the spouse in their child's new family unit may be coming from different socioeconomic status and not share the same sentiments, especially since the new family will have their immediate household needs and goals. This conflict of interest strains the relationship with the extended family. I have seen cases where the root cause of problems and divorce was the 'resource control' issue. People argue that the Bible says the parents are to leave an inheritance for their children and not look to a child's family for support, but every context is different, and I am not saying that this should be the norm. Yet, gifts, gifting and giving in the relationship sphere play an important role in finding, choosing and keeping the one.

Strategic giving

We already noted that you could give gifts for several reasons such as in appreciation. You can also

> There is a time to give gifts; there is a time to refuse gifts.

give to right wrongs or appease someone you have offended. When Jacob was returning home from self-exile and heard that his brother Esau was coming toward him with four hundred men, he was alarmed: *Jacob stayed where he was for the night. Then he selected these gifts from his possessions to present to his brother, Esau: 200 female goats, 20 male goats, 200 ewes, 20 rams, 30 female camels with their young, 40 cows, 10 bulls, 20 female donkeys, and 10 male donkeys. He divided these animals into herds and assigned each to different servants. Then he told his servants, "Go ahead of me with the animals, but keep some distance between the herds."*

He gave these instructions to the men leading the first group: "When my brother, Esau, meets you, he will ask, 'Whose servants are you? Where are you going? Who owns these animals?' You must reply, 'They belong to your servant Jacob, but they are a gift for his master Esau. Look, he is coming right behind us."... ...Jacob thought, "I will try to appease him by sending gifts ahead of me. When I see him in person, perhaps he will be friendly to me." So the gifts were sent on ahead, while Jacob himself spent that night in the camp.[120]

Jacob sent gifts ahead, and he did it strategically – in creative batches that would have softened even the hardest heart. It was a tough night for Jacob, but he knew his deliverance and success depended on the seed of gifts he would sow. The gifts and their presentation quelled any anger and hurt left in Esau from Jacob's deception. Jacob's giving melted Esau's hardened heart and dispelled whatever vengeful plans Esau had — especially since he had come to 'welcome' Jacob with an army. Jacob was wise. It takes wisdom to give strategically. I know people who gave and gave in the face of rejection until they won over the heart of their love interest. Your gift can prepare the heart of your intended to open to you or appreciate you more. When parental consent to get married is not provided, many have given to warm the hearts of parents or guardians of their prospective spouse. If you are convinced that this is the one for you, and with all the other principles working, then your gift should not be seen as a bribe but in the context of God's purpose for gifts.

However, one should be cautious in using gifts to wow or win over. People who do not have a pure heart often give with a wrong motive to influence the discretion and decision of the receiver. While you do not want to get married to someone who is stingy with their resources (and even justifies it), you must be careful of men or women who go out of their way to influence your decision about getting married to them through gifts.

A time to say no

There is a time to give gifts and a time to refuse gifts. There was a season when I was receiving all kinds of gifts. My girlfriends and I spent a lot of time evaluating and talking about the value, packaging, or the giver. I became even more confused about what I wanted in a marriage partner. People will go as far as offering you cars, a complete change of wardrobe, expensive trips, and it can all be so tempting. Even when you object and ask for a motive, the *gifter* may say, 'oh, it's just a simple gift, there is nothing behind it, I just want you to have it.' However, it is not that simple when it comes to relationships.

The heart is very deceitful, and people can even deceive themselves into believing that there is no motive for their actions unless they are true enough to themselves. In my Igbo ethnic group, a suitor's giving, and the 'weight' of the gifts are often used to indicate how serious they are and the kind of in-law they will be. And this viewpoint and expectation often put young couples under undue pressure.

You may need to come to a point where you decide to refuse gifts, even when it offends the receiver or giver. That stance will set you free to see clearly, who or what you do not want in a relationship. Further, receiving gifts from someone when you know in your heart that you do not intend to get married to them is greed and wickedness. Why lead them on?

The story is about Gehazi, Elisha's servant who was overtaken by the lure and pleasure of gifts. They were not living in luxury, and the gifts from Naaman would have certainly improved their wellbeing and estate, even if for a period. Moreover, they had worked for the gifts by curing Naaman of his illness? The gifts were well-deserved, Gehazi rationalized. Gifts could be justified as payment for service rendered, and in a relationship context, it could be the time you spent hearing out or entertaining a prospective wooer. There is also the problem of a *'chop my money'* frame of mind, re the popular song by P Square and friends, where greed and the desire to acquire more, wear the latest designs and keep up with the trend push individuals to give and receive gifts without recourse to the purpose of giving.

Well, after Gehazi surreptitiously took the gifts, Elisha said something that we can all take to heart. *Is this <u>the time</u> to take money or to accept clothes—or olive groves and vineyards, or flocks and herds, or male and female slaves? Naaman's leprosy will cling to you and to your descendants forever." Then Gehazi went from Elisha's presence and his skin was leprous—it had become as white as snow.*[121] He did not give any reason why it was not a good time to accept the gift, but it just was not the time. Gehazi paid dearly for his greed.

As Jacob sent his gift ahead with the sole purpose of placating Esau, people often subconsciously have errands, assignments, and sadly, in some cases, curses attached to their gifts. It would help if you were sensitive because sometimes gifts come with clauses unknown to you. Sometimes, accepting gifts is as good as giving your consent. Many have killed and sought revenge when they felt they had invested much in someone only to be rejected in the end. It will take a lot of discipline and self-control but be sensitive in giving or receiving gifts, and this applies to both males and females.

Courteously refusing unclassified gifts will send a strong message to the individual that you are waiting on God and will serve as a signal to God that you are relying solely on Him for your provision and waiting on Him for His choice for you. Refusing questionable gifts will avert any bitterness and the sense of entitlement, deception, or an impression that the interest is mutual. Even when you are in an awful situation with your finances, accepting gifts puts you in an awkward position and weakens your resolve and judgment regarding the choice of whom to get married to. Ask God to give you the grace to be disciplined and contented so as not to receive gifts from just anyone except the person with whom you will commit to marrying.

Ada and Chike

Ada's parents could not afford to send her to a university, so she started working at a clothing store after finishing high school. One rainy day, Chike walked into the store for shelter and began to examine a pair of jeans. Ada was there to help, they chatted a bit, and he asked for her phone number before he left. Chike would call Ada often, and a relationship began to evolve. Their phone calls would stretch into the night. His voice was the first she heard each morning and the last before she went to bed. He would often come by the store on his way home from his business or send lunch to her.

Ada enjoyed being the object of interest, and Chike was equal to the task with his age and wealth advantage. One day, Chike told Ada he would provide her with a scholarship for a college education. She was the perfect picture of a wife to him, and although he did not have the opportunity to get a college degree himself, he wanted to invest in her, even if for the sake of the future of the children they would have together. Ada was excited; her dreams had come true. Chike paid for her to attend lessons; she took the entrance exams and was successful. She enrolled in college, and Chike provided for everything she needed. Ada was soon popular and attracted a lot of friends because of how well-provided for that she was in school. Chike also went on to support Ada's family in many ways. He made her life easy. Ada's parents were always grateful, and they gave their unreserved approval to the relationship. Four years later, Ada would graduate.

Over time, she began to see how uncouth Chike was in his ways. She realized that her relationship with Chike would not work as her outlook on life had changed so much. As a college graduate, she felt that Chike did not fit the picture of her new status. When Chike began to discuss wedding plans, she said she was unsure she wanted to go ahead. She spoke to her parents about it, but they rebuked her for being so ungrateful after all he had done for their family and asked her to consider returning the favor by marrying him. Ada knew this relationship was heading for the rocks, but she wanted to please Chike and her parents.

Conflicts began soon after they were married. She found herself trying to correct Chike and make him act more educated. Reacting, Chike would always remind her that he met her when she had nothing in life, and he had made her what she had become. With the flawed mindset about marriage, everything — sex, communication, finances, conception - proved to be challenging. One day, Ada called her mum, crying and complaining that she was not enjoying her marriage. Her mum told her that there was no perfect marriage and that she should continue to pray and have a solid heart to endure the trials of marriage. In response to Ada's rejection, Chike became an entirely different person, despising the woman he once adored. Ada now says she would have preferred to be without a college education than be stuck in a sad marriage.

Love Gives

Gifts are a powerful accessory in finding and choosing the one and can work for or against the process. Gifts are a sign of the heart, commitment, and motive of the prospective spouse. Giving shows that the individual is thoughtful and mindful of you. A life of giving transcends the wooing period to courtship and influences how individuals give of themselves, their resources, body, or time through the eventual marriage. A life of giving defines you, and a habit of giving fosters the confidence of the prospective one to know that you will be in their corner in a time of need, and should you choose to embark on a marriage relationship with them.

Giving can be sacrificial and requires a level of selflessness which is important in relationships. God is the ultimate Giver; He gave His most precious gift, His only Son, Jesus Christ, as a sacrifice for the world's sins. For God so loved the world that He gave - Love gives. Just as Christ gave himself for the Church, those in relationships or wanting to enter into one need to cultivate a giving heart: *Husbands, love your wives, just as Christ also loved the church and gave Himself for her… So husbands ought to love their own wives as their own bodies; he who loves his wife loves himself.*[122]

Chapter 9
The principle of service

"Service is the rent we pay for being. It is the very purpose of life, and not something you do in your spare time."

- Marian Wright Edelman

Brian and Elsie met three years ago while on a short-term mission trip in Guatemala. Brian and Elsie had taken time off work to volunteer with the team. The mission trip that was supposed to end after the three-month stint lingered, and they found themselves still serving together with the group for another year. There was so much to do; Elsie was busy in the soup kitchen helping widows and orphans while Brian was engaged in a nearby school teaching young boys the English language. Brian's parents were missionaries, and he had gone on several trips with them, but this was his first trip alone without them. Elsie became excited about missions after an Australian missionary visited their youth group at her church.

> *Fewer instances lead us to or attract our prospective spouses to us than the place of service.*

While on the trip, the team prayed every morning and evening besides having lunch together and planning meetings. Brian and Elsie were in different groups but met each day. Brian watched Elsie serve and was amazed at how much love she had for the people in her care. Brian had never been in a relationship and did not think the mission field was a great place to begin. He kept his thoughts about Elsie to himself but thought about her the whole time.

At the end of the service period, there was an urgent request for more volunteers for another mission team going to Madagascar, and surprisingly, both Elsie and Brian signed up. Brian was excited that Elsie would be on the same team as him. Brian began to think that this was providence bringing them together again. He became convinced that the extended service opportunity in Madagascar and being on the same team was not a coincidence. When they got to Madagascar, Brian did not hold back his intentions; he told Elsie he had been praying about her and asked if she would mind his coming to her parents to ask for her hand in marriage when they got back to the states. He said that he wanted to walk in his parents' footsteps to be a full-time missionary -was that in any way part of her dreams? Elsie was elated; she liked Brain but was not thinking about a deep relationship now. She had been thinking about giving more of herself and her time to full-time missions– at least for a season of her life. With Brian's intention out in the open, the three months in Madagascar were different for the two of them. In their new-found interest and sense of joint mission, the service felt more fulfilling.

After they left the island, they got engaged. Brian's parents were excited when he shared the news; they had been praying that he would meet a prospective spouse whose mission aligned with his. This was an answer to prayers. Several months later, Brian and Elsie got married.

Fewer circumstances will lead you to or attract your prospective spouse to you than the place of service. Do you desire to find or be found quickly by God's choice for you? Then busy yourself serving your life's purpose. What type of life are you living today? How do you serve the people that interact with you daily? What makes you stand out from others? How do you plan to leave an impact and impression, not in terms of your looks, in the minds of those who encounter you? Do you have a quality of being available to serve others when needed or when it is in your power to do so?

Service is a duty we owe

To serve is the act of helping someone, lending a helping hand, or aiding another. It is a 'doing' word. A servant is an attendant, a waiter, who seeks to satisfy the needs of others.

Service is a duty we owe. Marian Wright Edelman said that *"service is the rent we pay for being. It is the very purpose of life, and not something you do in your spare time"*. Service is our reason for being. We each have different gifts and abilities. We are most fulfilled, and our gifts are at their best when used to benefit others. Peter said, *"God has given each of you a gift from His great variety of spiritual gifts. Use them well to serve one another."*[123] Service attracts the approval and favor of God and fosters divine activity in your life. The story is told of Cornelius' whose acts of service attracted God's attention and saving grace. Each time you are serving, God is working in and through you: *For it is God who works in you, both to will and to work for his good pleasure*[124].

The strength to serve

She went down to the spring, filled her jug, and came back up. The servant ran to meet her and said, "Please, can I have a sip of water from your jug?"

She said, "Certainly, drink!" And she held the jug so that he could drink. When he had satisfied his thirst she said, "I'll get water for your camels, too, until they've drunk their fill." She promptly emptied her jug into the trough and ran back to the well to fill it, and she kept at it until she had watered all the camels.[125]

Rebekah was an amazing and strong woman who had a great heart. She was not idle; instead, she was busy with her assignments. First, she had the task of going to the well to get water for her family. She served in her family. As the text noted, she got to the well on time, too, indicating that she managed her time effectively. When Eliezer asked for some water, she obliged him and gave him water to quench his thirst. She was kind and considerate of the needs of others. Did you wonder that the servant and his entourage did not travel with their water jugs to draw water, or could it be that they did not have access to the community's well as strangers from another land? In any case, Rebekah offered to help and went the extra mile to give water to his entourage and camels.

Many have analyzed what a feat it was for Rebekah to serve Abraham's servant, Eliezer. A camel consumes about ten gallons of water. Rebekah would

> A servant is an attendant or waiter, who seeks to satisfy the needs of other. To serve is the act of helping someone, lending a helping hand

have had to draw and discharge the equivalent of approximately twenty, five-liter plastic cans of water (3,381 oz), making about fifteen trips to the well. What a task. By the way, how could Eliezer and the men he traveled with sit and watch while this lady did all the work, expending all that energy to serve them? Maybe they were so exhausted from their journey or, as suggested earlier, did not have access to the city's well or perhaps, testing her mettle. Pray for and seek to build your strength, physically and in your inner man so that in life and in your day of blessing, you will always rise to the occasion.

The humility to serve

Would you (male or female) be willing to offer to serve while others sit around watching, doing nothing? Would you not have some reservations? Do they think you are a slave or what? Yet, Rebekah humbly served this entourage. She did not consider her reputation as a leading lady from a great family. Genuine service, especially in relationships, often leaves you vulnerable: your service may not be accepted or appreciated even when you are giving your best from your heart. The response or remarks from others may be condescending. But once you understand the power of serving others, you will not mind the naysayers.

Rebekah set the precedence. Her service is the basis of the excellence and example she is to all today. But why did she do it? What prompted her to kindly give him water and, on second thought, decide to take up the grueling task to provide for the camels as well? Was she trying to burn some calories? What was in it for her? This was just a person who took pleasure in making life easier for others. She would do whatever it would take to bring a smile on the face of another person, especially a weary traveler. The words of her lips were full of tender kindness. Rebekah worked hard, and I imagine that it was her lifestyle. Excellence, they say, is not an act but a habit, since you are what you repeatedly do. What a price to pay to be singled out as the one who would continue the greatest family marriage dynasty. She served without even knowing that something was at stake, epitomizing service at its best.

It takes humility to serve, not considering your high status, accomplishments, or pedigree. Everyone has a measure of pride, and this can impede service. The downside of pride is that it can be camouflaged, especially in situations where people, in false humility, refuse to be served. 'I'm fine, I've got this, oh, don't bother, I can take care of myself" — they say, when in truth, they need the help. Some people flaunt a self-made, and independent presentation of themselves. However, the truth is that while independence is good, interdependence is greater. As you serve, be willing to be served.

Further, if you are self-conscious and think about what people will say, you may not serve. Humility, deadness-to-self, and selflessness go hand in hand with service: *"You must have the same attitude that Christ Jesus had. Though He was God, He did not think of equality with God as something to cling to. Instead, He gave up His divine privileges; took the humble position of a slave, and was born as a human being. When he appeared in human form, he humbled himself in obedience to God and died a criminal's death on a cross."*[126]

Acceptable service

Selfless - There are ways to serve. Genuine service is selfless. You do not help others to receive an acknowledgment, to be celebrated, or to be given an award for the good you do, especially in or toward a relationship. If the applause does not come, serve anyway. You do not serve to feed your pride. Paul wrote, *"Don't act out of selfish ambition or be conceited, instead, humbly think of others as being better than yourselves".*[127] Acceptable acts of service are laced with the right thoughts, intentions, and attitudes.

> Serving puts you in a position to lead, to find and be found. A life of service will distinguish you and cause you to stand out.

A lifestyle - Further, a life of service is not a one-off event; you cannot choose a day not to serve or do good deeds. Every opportunity, to do good, is a good opportunity. When Rebekah woke up that morning, she did not know that her routine act of kindness and service would be a setup for a divine connection. *So then, as we have opportunity, let* us do good to everyone, and especially to those who are of the household of faith[128].

With diligence - You are to serve with diligence, not lazily or reluctantly. Diligence in service ensures that you are well resourced, a vital ingredient for a successful relationship. Having more than enough (resources) makes finding and choosing the one easier. You can do more: *The thoughts of the diligent tend only to plenteousness; but of everyone that is hasty only to want. Another version says: "Good planning and hard work lead to prosperity, but hasty shortcuts lead to poverty".*[129] Rebekah was a person of action and got things done. She was diligent and a leader that would become the mother of nations: *The hand of the diligent shall bear rule: while the slothful shall be put to forced labor*[130].

Not unto man – For your wellbeing and that of others, serve as unto God. People will be ungrateful, may not appreciate you, may even misunderstand your motives, or backbite you. To safeguard against bitterness in living a life of service, serve as unto God, not unto man: *(serve) not with eyeservice, as men-pleasers, but as bondservants of Christ, doing the will of God from the heart, with goodwill doing service, as to the Lord, and not to men, knowing that whatever good anyone does, he will receive the same from the Lord, whether he is a slave or free.*[131]

Service is a principle with benefits. Putting your hands and mind to good purpose and enterprise before marriage can help you build up savings - material and spiritual. Would it not rather be wonderful that, as a young couple, you have enough resources saved up to ensure that when you have young children, you are available for them rather than having to work all hours to make ends meet?

Service is a cure for loneliness

'Then the LORD God said, "It is not good for the man to be alone. I will make a helper who is right for him."[132] Service is a cure for loneliness.

A helper, one to serve alongside, was given because he was alone. When you get about serving or volunteering, especially with others, there is no room for pity parties from loneliness. Helping

> *True service especially in relationships requires that you allow yourself to be vulnerable: your service may not be accepted or appreciated even when you are at your best*

or serving is intricately linked to companionship and your mental well-being. Rebekah exhibited this primary quality from the onset. And as with every principle, service works both ways, equally applying to the man and the woman.

Service sets you up as a leader

Are you serving or sitting — waiting to be served? Leadership is about helping others. Serving puts you in a position to lead, to find, and be found. A person that is always willing to serve for the good of others is a leader. Jacob served while he lived in the house of Laban, and the man was excited to extend the relationship. Joseph served so well that he was promoted from the prison to the palace. Your service distinguishes you and makes it easier for you to find love and be found: *Seest thou a man diligent in his business? He shall stand before kings; he shall not stand before mean men.*[133] Your service highlights you and sets you up for recognition. *The hand of the diligent shall bear rule: while the slothful shall be put to forced labor.* Another translation put it this way: "*Work hard and become a leader; be lazy and become a slave.*" Your service is the true measure of leadership. Rebekah's service and hard work defined her and were instrumental in her being a partner with God in fulfilling the covenant God had with Abraham.

What problems are you resolving? Where and when is help needed that you are volunteering yourself? If you have discovered your assignment, how are you fulfilling it to make a difference in your sphere of influence? Are you merely occupying space on earth, or are you contributing? *But Jesus called them together and said, "You know that the rulers in this world lord it over their people, and officials flaunt their authority over those under them. But among you it will be different. Whoever wants to be a leader among you must be your servant, and whoever wants to be first among you must become your slave.*[134]

Rebekah was not serving for a reward, yet the blessing found her. She used her gift of wisdom, strength, and encouragement to help others. In the place of service, Rebekah was seen and connected to her marital destiny.

Service is protective

Besides service to humanity and your spouse, your service to God is the ultimate. The first service required of man is service to God: *"You must serve only the Lord your God. If you do, I will bless you with food and water, and I will protect you from illness*[135]. Service is protective; service attracts blessings from God. Can God testify that you are serving Him? Serving God is doing whatever you do to bring the will and rule of God to bear in your sphere of influence, *so that the knowledge of the glory of God, overs the earth as the waters cover the sea*[136].

There are also opportunities for service in the house of God. God equips people and expects that these gifts also benefit His place of worship: *"The Lord has gifted Bezalel, Oholiab, and the other skilled craftsmen with wisdom and ability to perform any task involved in building the sanctuary. Let them construct and furnish the Tabernacle, just as the Lord has commanded."*[137] As with the principle of gifts, no service is too big or small. You do not have to be "seen" or acknowledged while serving. *Whatever your hands find to do, do with all your heart and might…*[138]

Service is rewarding

Every effort you expend for others is a seed sown. Life has a principle of seedtime and harvest time for all we do, and service to others is not excluded. There is a promise of rewards for your acts of service: *And let us not grow weary of doing good, for in due season we will reap, if we do not give up.*[139] How heartwarming to know that the One that sees your heart of service will reward you! There are rewards for every labor. Givers (of themselves) never lack.

Jesus was rewarded for His servant leadership and promoted. God gave Him a position of exceptional honor, the name honored above all other names: "*In your relationships with one another, have the same mindset as Christ Jesus …Who made himself nothing … by taking the very nature of a servant [service], … he humbled himself …Therefore God exalted him to the highest place and gave him the name that is above every name.*"[140] As a result of Jesus's life of service and humility, God elevated Him.

Service can be tasking

You are often told that you do not get tired or feel the burden of work if you are in your calling, that it is like a hobby. However, service can be tasking; if you do not care for yourself, you can experience burnout. Rebekah can tell. Service can wear you out. Be sure to take care of yourself, but do not stop serving. You can never tell which last act of service will be the one that is needed to save a life! Do not wear out, be refreshed! *And let us not grow weary of doing good.*[141]

And there is a provision for your restoration as you serve, selfcare in God's presence. David was a chief servant, and he had this to say:

The Lord is my shepherd; I have all that I need. He lets me rest in green meadows; he leads me beside peaceful streams. He renews my strength:[142] God restores your soul with rivers of living water.

The greater life

Finding the love of your life, your eventual marriage, promotions, blessings, and the quality of your life are dependent on the life of excellence and service you render. The greater life is the life that is poured out in service to others. To find and choose the love of your life, you must operate from the life and principle of service. The principle of service expects that your life is lived to leave an impact on the lives of others. Service is the giving of yourself. Service makes you stand out. If you desire to get married or be a leader, watch out – you are signing up for a life of service. Are you a servant? When you are with family and friends, and there are needs to be met, are they pleased that you are there because your presence assures loving and collaborative service? That is the stuff marriage is made of.

Part III
To be, before you do and have

The most important work you will ever do, no matter what occupation you end up choosing is called "working on yourself"
— Mark Fisher

Chapter 10
The principle of dedication

Meanwhile, Isaac, whose home was in the Negev, had returned from Beer-lahai-roi. One evening as he was walking and meditating in the fields, he looked up and saw the camels coming. [143]

Daniel and Debbie got married eighteen months after meeting at a friend's wedding. Daniel attended a college in Accra, but Deborah schooled at a university in Lagos. They had individually decided when they were teenagers, and after giving their lives to Jesus, that they would be celibate until they got married. Neither had been in a previous relationship.

Before he met Debbie, Daniel would pray and fast for his prospective spouse once a week, and on her part, Debbie always prayed for her future. Neither wanted to take a chance to get married to just anyone. Debbie had seen her mum struggle to raise her and her three brothers without their father. She vowed to do something different for her family; she resolved to marry a godly man and raise her children in a more functional home.

When Debbie and Daniel met, they were surprised to discover that they shared so much in common. They wanted a spouse who feared the Lord and who was passionate about the things of God. They had been attending the same annual youth camp for many years but never met each other. Debbie was not the most beautiful woman, but Daniel could not stop glancing her way. Even though Daniel knew in his heart that Debbie could be the one for him, he did not share this with her until after two months. When he finally shared his intentions with her, she asked for time to pray about it.

In their marriage, Daniel and Debbie continue to enjoy their relationship, and their marriage has been a blessing to so many people. Many people wonder how Daniel and Debbie's marriage has remained stable over the years. People who meet them for the first time often think they must pretend to be having such a good marriage. There must be more than meets the eye, they think. Daniel and Debbie's relationship is the expected and predictable outcome of the principle of dedication. They had taken time to grow from within, building their lives on the truth of God's word, cultivating, and bearing the fruit of the Spirit - *But the Holy Spirit produces this kind of fruit in our lives: love, joy, peace, patience, kindness, goodness, faithfulness, gentleness, and self-control. There is no law against these things!*[144] Their kind of success in finding and choosing the love of their life was inevitable and predictable.

Your commitments

The principle of dedication is about the compounding power of a life committed to God and His ways. You are not perfect, but you have the grace to thrive in your relationship. We see an expression of dedication in the life of the prospective spouse, Isaac. Isaac was out in the fields in meditation. Meditation is a spiritual practice, expressed in many words such as solitude, muttering, musing, reflection, worship, or talking to God. Meditation is an act or expression of the life of dedication and art of prayer. During meditation, you focus and concentrate on God and His words. Meditation fosters a connection to the spirit realm where God, who is Spirit lives.

Isaac had a habit of meditating and was committed to God's promise to Abraham to be fulfilled in his generation. He was committed to his relationship with God: *Meanwhile, Isaac, whose home was in the Negev, had returned from Beer-lahai-roi. One evening as he was walking and meditating in the fields, he looked up and saw the camels coming.*[145]

Dedication expresses your connection to the principle of divine activity. As you spend time with God in quietness and solitude, you step into the world with a clear, sound mind, full of peace. Dedication leads to a centered, grounded life. When you live life from a place of dedication to God, you may not have all the answers and solutions to your day, but there is a peace and confidence that you are on a journey with God: *The way of the righteous is like the first gleam of dawn, which shines ever brighter until the full light of day.*[146] You are not afraid of tomorrow because you are walking with the One who knows and is in charge of tomorrow. *If you move close to God, God will come close to you.*[147] God said, *'Ask me and I will tell you remarkable secrets you do not know about things to come.*[148]

You become friends with God through dedication, and friends share secrets. God is a revealer of secrets. You will never be completely sure that the one you are choosing is the right one, but God will give you the peace to go ahead, nevertheless. He will lead you toward and speak to your heart about your spouse. Because Isaac sought

> The principle of dedication has to do with the compounding interest and power of a life committed to God and His ways

the quietness of God's presence, he became a friend of God. Isaac hoped that when the prospective bride came, he would be sure that they were right for each other, God's Spirit speaking to his heart: *The Spirit Himself bears witness with our spirit*[149]. The principle of dedication awakens your recognition. There is a 'quickening' and opening of your eyes to recognize the one that God has chosen for you.

Isaac and Rebekah were dedicated and committed to God. They both had deep roots in the faith. Isaac fellowshipped with God and had a habit of meditation as his father Abraham, the friend of God, must have taught him. Abraham, called a prophet by God, received many revelations about his future and destiny.

Dedication and your spirituality

The principle of dedication is also known as the triangle principle and is a critical consideration in finding the love of your life, making the commitment, and enjoying your union over the long haul. The triangle typifies the man and woman at the base, reaching up and joining at the apex in God. As each partner seeks and grows closer to God, both meet in a perfect and stronger union at the peak, God. However, if they grow horizontally toward each other at the base, without God in the picture, the self and flesh will rule the relationship, and this will result in manifold conflicts because the relationship will be all about the self — selfish, and being human, full of faults and imperfection.

Focusing on self and putting one's interest above the partner is the greatest enemy of relationships. But if the partners grow toward God, they will meet in His perfect love to become a three-fold cord that cannot be broken: *Likewise, two people lying close together can keep each other warm. But how can one be warm alone? A person standing alone can be attacked and defeated, but two can stand back-to-back and conquer. Three are even better, for a triple-braided cord is not easily broken.*[150] A life of dedication enables you to take on the character of God, and God is love.

Dedication is different from prayer in that many people would pray "fire brigade" prayers, which are prayers prayed in times of great need, trials, or trouble which God in His infinite mercy answers. Some people fast and attend every prayer and miracle service, but they are over with Him once God answers. Do you pray only when you have a major decision to take, have an exam, an interview, or face life-threatening sickness?

The principle of dedication goes further – it is a lifestyle, a culture, a way of being. When you are dedicated and have that regular time with God, you stay in fellowship with Him, in His presence; you do not step out of the relationship. It has been said, "falling in love is easy but staying in love requires a plan." The principle of dedication is "the plan" that ensures that you choose the right partner and have daily grace for the pressures of a relationship and that your love for each other will last a lifetime.

The principle of dedication implies that if you are dedicated to God, you can count on God's guidance in finding and choosing the love of your life and the wisdom to be a great spouse. Years back, James Souter wrote in the Date Magazine that the possibility of getting married to your heart's desire (who is God's will for you) is directly proportional to the closeness and relationship you share with God. You can take that counsel to heart and be assured as you live dedicated to God, that it will be well with you in choosing a marriage partner. Dedication to God results in a sensitive heart both to God, your inner person, and your prospective partner. A tender heart has an increased ability to hear God speak. You become more intuitive and discerning. In addition, a person who is dedicated or committed to God will know God, have a fear of Him, and seek His will before they act. More likely, a person devoted to God will want to work in the relationship's best interest.

Do you want a positive relationship? Then a life of dedication that promotes the presence of God in your life is critical. If you seek a partner who will, together with you, pursue joy all the days of your marriage, then consider their dedication and commitment to God. You will both continually find joy in God's presence, and that is a source of strength for your relationship journey: *In Your presence is fullness of joy; At Your right hand are pleasures forevermore.*[151] And again: *For the joy of the Lord is your strength!"*[152]

Another example of dedication is the case of Ruth. One of the significant steps in Ruth finding the love of her life was her dedication to God. Her response to Naomi was essentially a confession of her faith: *But Ruth replied, "Don't ask me to leave you and turn back. Wherever you go, I will go; wherever you live, I will live. Your people will be my people, and your God will be my God.*[153] The most important thing she was doing here was committing her life to God. Ruth gave her life to God. Ruth's dedication to God was the primary reason for her move to Israel. Later, Boaz would attest to her life of dedication: *Boaz replied. "But I also know about everything you have done for your mother-in-law since the death of your husband. I have heard how you left your father and mother and your own land to live here among complete strangers. May the Lord, the God of Israel, under whose wings you have come to take refuge, reward you fully for what you have done."*[154] Dedication is coming to take refuge in God, who is love. And did God reward her! She got married to a great man who was equally dedicated to God. And talking of a great family marriage dynasty - yes, she is named in the lineage of the Christ.

> The principle of dedication states that if you are dedicated to God, you can count on God's guidance in the choice of a spouse and wisdom to be a great spouse

Someone has said that if you do not stand for something, you will fall for anything. Everyone is dedicated to something or passionate about something unless their life no longer makes sense to them – and that is not a good place to be. What are you or the person you are interested in dedicated to? You will need to clarify that? First, check what takes over 50% of the individual's time.

Further, without a life of dedication, it is easy to tire of someone and seek another attraction. Lasting love starts by being dedicated to God, the best practice of all. When you are dedicated to God, as you would need to be dedicated to the love of your life, you will realize that there are some no-go areas, some dealbreakers that will ruin your relationship with God or your love. Dedication makes it easy for you to set up the boundaries in your life. You must decide and know where you stand in your dedication to God and in your walk with Him.

Primarily, Jesus divided the sum of our dedications to either God or money (materiality) – you spend most of your time thinking or meditating about the object of your dedication: *"No servant can serve two masters; for either he will hate the one and love the other, or else he will be loyal to the one and despise the other. You cannot serve God and mammon."*[155] Further, *"for where your treasure is, there your heart will be also."*[156] When you think of all the beautiful words that are used to express endearment, then you realize what a treasure your love interest is and why your heart is there. The principle of dedication is about making that clarification and practicing it.

Make God a priority in all your dedications and passions, the numero uno. Dedication requires a level of discipline. Discipline is vital in setting yourself up to find and choose the right one for you and help you and your love manage the roads ahead. Your dedication will help to build up your spiritual life. Life in the Spirit provides you with the grace to understand different perspectives, navigate challenges and win, which is essential when two people plan to come together to form a new unit.

Chapter 11
The principle of purity

"Purity prepares the soul for love, and love confirms the soul in purity"

– John Henry Newman

Tony and Mercy met at a downtown café. They got married two years after. Mercy had a sexually active life and had been involved in many relationships in the past. Tony was looking forward to their month-long honeymoon but noticed that Mercy was not as excited. He thought she was exhausted by all the wedding preparations. The honeymoon quickly went by, and they began their life together.

Tony could not help feeling that Mercy was emotionally disconnected from him. The exhaustion he thought he saw was beginning to look more like boredom. On her side, Mercy felt that Tony was not as adventurous and satisfying as the other men she had been in relationships with. It was not long before they gradually drifted away from each other, seeking other pastimes to occupy them. Mercy began to disrespect Tony, and this harmed their relationship. While Tony was brooding and trying to figure out the direction of the relationship, Mercy started hanging out with some old friends. She accused Tony of being immature and not ready for marriage. Mercy loved Tony, did not like how their marriage was evolv-

> *Purity comes from God, when a heart is cleansed by the blood of Jesus, and with the help of the Holy Spirit, you receive the grace to live a life of purity.*

ing, but could not help herself. Tony could not lay his finger on what exactly was going wrong with the marriage.

The relationship went from bad to worse. Tony decided to share his frustrations with his uncle, who suggested meeting with a marriage counselor. Mercy did not agree to meet a counselor; she preferred some space from Tony to fix their issues. There were nights she would not sleep in their room. It was tough for Tony to accept this new pattern in their relationship, but he did his best to keep up with the quirks - praying and hoping things would change.

Mercy was moved to a new unit at work and began to report to a new manager. Mercy's new manager noticed her poor performance at work and invited Mercy to her office one morning. Out of the blues, she asked, 'How's your relationship with your spouse?' Mercy was surprised at the question, and before she could gather herself to respond, tears rolled down her cheeks. 'Not great,' Mercy replied, and they spent the next forty minutes chatting quietly. Mercy's manager was a woman of faith who led her to the Lord, and Mercy rededicated her heart to Jesus. They prayed that the Spirit of God would break every imagery, memory, and attachment to past relationships from her life. For the first time in a long time, Mercy felt whole, clean, and free. God had lifted the burden of the weight from the past off her life. How she wanted to make it right in her marriage! Mercy could not wait to share the news with Tony that night. He was surprised about the turn of events, but he was glad to be reconnected to his wife. It was tough beginning again, but they began to work at it.

Purity is an attribute of God

Purity is an important attribute or value of God, and He created us in His likeness and image. God is pure and holy and wants us to be holy just as He is. Purity in body (physical), soul (thoughts), and spirit (heart) is of utmost importance if you will find and marry the best one for you. Have you ever heard the phrase; cleanliness is next to godliness? It was a 17th-century proverb used to promote hygiene or 'clenlyness,' at that time. Keep the phrase close to mind as we explore purity. The principle of purity implies that if you live a pure life, you will be close to God and easily discern God's voice in finding and choosing the love of your life.

Rebekah was a virgin when Abraham's servant met her, which is desirable in choosing a marriage partner. She was described as chaste, a virgin, whom no man had touched: *The girl was a very attractive virgin. No man had ever had sexual intercourse with her…*[157] She was working in the public domain, exposed to others, some of whom may have admired and sought after her. How could Eliezer have known about her virtues? Was it from her dressing, demeanor, or had someone hinted? Hard to tell. But this was a notable factor in finding Isaac's bride.

There is a festering moral decadence in society. Many young people experience intentional or unintended events that make the concept of marrying as virgins seem almost impossible. Movies make promiscuity commonplace and acceptable. Young people who desire to be chaste are mocked as prudish, slow, and old fashioned. Peer pressure and the glaring influence of the media ridicule the virtue of purity. The essence and possibility of staying pure before marriage is now being debated.

However, purity of spirit, soul, and body as an individual makes you better for relationship. Purity helps you to discern people quickly. As pure water is clear, so purity makes your eyes clear, and as a clear mirror, you are more discerning: *"Your eye is like a lamp that provides light for your body. When your eye is healthy, your whole body is filled with light.*[158]

Purity and sex

God's original plan is that men and women marry without sexual relationships before marriage. Nothing corrupts or destroys purity and attractiveness as much as sexual immorality.

> There is nothing that corrupts attractiveness as sexual immorality that drains the life and beauty of God from your life.

Sex outside of marriage drains the life and beauty of God from your life. Many women have said that they always felt cheap, dirty, and left with low self-esteem when they were involved in sexual relationships outside of marriage. Paul wrote, *"God's will is for you to be holy, so stay away from all sexual sin. Then each of you will control his own body and live in holiness and honor—not in lustful passion like the pagans who do not know God and his ways.*"[159]

A person who desires to find and keep the love of their life must make a personal commitment to stay pure. The devil continues to sell the lie to this generation that sex when you want it, with whomever and however is ok. Rather than follow the trend, seek to stand out. You can decide not to go with the crowd. There is so much to gain and nothing to lose from getting married as a virgin or choosing to stay pure till marriage if you are no longer a virgin. There are special assignments reserved for men and women who have kept themselves pure – special utensils reserved for honorable use. God chose a virgin to be the mother of Jesus. When Vashti was no longer queen, the king sought for a virgin to replace her, and Esther fit the bill[160]. Paul wrote: *In a wealthy home, some utensils are made of gold and silver, and some are made of wood and clay. The expensive utensils are used for special occasions, and the cheap ones are for everyday use. If you keep yourself pure, you will be a special utensil for honorable use. Your life will be clean, and you will be ready for the Master to use you for every good work.*[161] This is the principle of purity at work.

Purity qualifies you for a life of honor. There will always be value for your commitment to a life of purity of spirit, soul, and body. While finding and keeping the love of your life, no matter what popular culture says, God will always have a special provision for men and women who keep themselves pure for marriage.

On the God side

While purity or virginity is most often used to refer to, and deride women, God expects the same level of chastity from both men and women. Sometimes, men are subjected to less than acceptable standards of purity than women, where only the woman's actions are judged, and the man gets away with his lifestyle. I also know women who have complained that though they kept themselves, they ended up with unworthy men as husbands and wondered if it was indeed worth their while to have stayed pure. Just keep being good, I say. You live for God and will give an account to Him someday. God's parameters and rewards are different from yours. While we fall short, it does not change God's standards.

In addition, staying away from sexual relationships before marriage is not enough; God sees and knows if you enjoy secret sins like impure thoughts or vices such as indulging in pornography or masturbation.

Purity is living a holy and wholesome life; it is not morality or legalism. Sexual sin with self or someone that you are not married to is a source of impurity that has spiritual and physical consequences. Paul wrote: *Don't you realize that your bodies are actually everyone parts of Christ? Should a man take his body, which is part of Christ, and join it to a prostitute? Never! And don't you realize that if a man (or woman) joins himself to a prostitute, he (or she) becomes one body with her (him)? For the Scriptures say, "The two are united into one." But the person who is joined to the Lord is one spirit with him.* In another place, he warns, '*Run from sexual sin! No other sin so clearly affects the body as this one does. For sexual immorality is a sin against your own body. Don't you realize that your body is the temple of the Holy Spirit, who lives in you and was given to you by God? You do not belong to yourself, for God bought you with a high price. So you must honor God with your body.*' [162]

During sex, partners merge their bodies, souls, and spirits. So apart from the joining and physical pleasure (or not) that is associated with sex, souls and spirits unite for good or bad. The two become one, and there are transfers and mingling of destinies beyond the transference of bodily fluids. There is a clinging beyond the physical that happens, and this often results in a soul tie. You are never quite the same after (except you consciously pray yourself out or break those ties). You carry bits of the positives and negatives from intercourse in previous sexual relationships into the next.

Take, for instance, Jacob's daughter, Dinah: *And when Shechem the son of Hamor the Hivite, prince of the country, saw her, he took her, and lay with her, and defiled her. And his <u>soul clave</u> unto Dinah the daughter of Jacob, and he loved the damsel, and spake kindly unto the damsel. And Shechem spake unto his father Hamor, saying, Get me this damsel to wife.*[163] After Shechem raped Dinah, his soul clave or clung to her. What he experienced afterward was not love but rather a soul tie. The whole affair was distasteful to her family, and moreover, any relationship with him would have been an unequal yoke.

Sexual sin results in scars and unwanted consequences, so if you want to have a great marriage, run from sexual immorality. Marriages are more successful when you enter without any baggage from previous relationships. 'Baggage' refers to all the exchanges, disappointments, wrongs, scars from past relationships, intergenerational or current trauma. Everyone has a past and one story or the other to tell, but if you repent of sexual sins as with other sins, God is faithful and fair to forgive you of all unrighteousness. God always makes a way of escape. You can start afresh on a clean, healed slate.

You can be renewed, restored, and have a fresh start. The blood of the Lamb, Jesus cleanses from sin, for *He has removed our sins as far from us as the east is from the west*[164]. He promises to give you a new slate to begin a new journey. *Therefore, if anyone is in Christ, he is a new creation; old things have passed away; behold, all things have become new.*[165] When you come to God renouncing every tie from the past, His power sets you free, and you can enjoy the benefits of a new union with your life partner.

Secondary virginity

A godly foundation and a heart that seeks after God will keep you pure until marriage. If you have already lost your virginity, no problem. There is secondary virginity. Secondary virginity comes when you ask God for forgiveness; renew your covenant with Him, decide to remain pure in words, thoughts, and actions – and particularly with sexual relationships. Whether you are or are no longer a virgin, you can decide to keep yourself pure until you get married. As you do, God will honor you, help you, restore, and reward you with the joys of sexual purity in marriage. Realize that there are virgins, either because they were careful to keep themselves pure, avoided penetrative intercourse, or because they did not get an opportunity to adventure. One can be a virgin, yet they may be wicked or impure in their hearts. God is not unjust. He knows and sees it all.

> *Secondary virginity comes when you ask God for forgiveness; renew your covenant with Him; choose and decide to remain pure in words, thoughts, and actions, especially concerning sexual relationships, until you get married*

There are several ways that those not married can keep themselves pure and avoid the traps of sex before marriage. Paul wrote asking Timothy *"to abstain from all appearance of evil"*[166]—to stay away from situations or environments that make him vulnerable to sexual sin, and to *"Flee also youthful lusts"* [167]— to run as fast as his feet could carry him when faced with the temptation to get fresh with the opposite sex. People may laugh at you, but you have a goal, you have something precious you want to preserve unto God, to please Him and, to assure clarity of mind in finding the love of your life.

Jacob's daughter, Dinah spent time with friends about town – the same company that her uncle Esau had been attracted to that led to his losing his heritage. These were the same company that Abraham had instructed Eliezer against while he searched for a spouse for Isaac. Dinah was raped. The young man could not get over her and was prepared to do anything to get married to her but was that the plan for her life? There were fatal consequences, including bloodshed. Sometimes, you may want to stay pure before marriage, but a terrible incident like rape or abuse happens. Struggling with the trauma of sexual abuse or addiction can be daunting. But God has healing for anyone that needs it today.

The principle of purity in choosing a life partner means you must consciously guard your spirit, soul, and body. It involves consecrating your life. While purity is not a tangible thing, purity makes you attractive. With the help of the Holy Spirit, you receive the grace to live a life of purity. Through Christ Jesus, the Spirit gives you the freedom and power to live a holy life and sets us free: *For the law of the Spirit of life in Christ Jesus hath made me free from the law of sin and death.* [168]. It is a blessing to be pure: Jesus says, '*you're blessed when you get your inside world—your mind and heart—put right. Then you can see God in the outside world*'. Another translation says, '*God blesses those whose hearts are pure, for they will see God.*'[169]

Chapter 12
The principle of focus

Focus is the lens through which the determined explore the beautiful thing called life...

- Robb Thompson

Martha had just begun her first term in medical school when she met James, a resident at the teaching hospital. They got into an on-and-off relationship, enjoying each other's company, and would spend lots of their little free time together for weeks on end. James was brilliant, a great role model, and inspired Martha. Martha's friends were concerned about her relationship with James but did not want to get between them. It was taking up all her time, even when she was not with him in person. Nonetheless, they looked like they would make such a great match.

Martha and James were no longer dating at the end of her first year. She spent the summer holidays alone and did not keep in touch with him. James wooed her back at the start of the next school year, and as she got more involved with him, her grades began to fall. James was even more attractive now as many of the new girls in the program seemed interested in him. Martha felt honored to be the 'chosen one.' She felt she had to spend more time with James, whose program now consisted of clinical rounds rather than intensive study. Martha spent a lot of time thinking about each encounter with James and planning how to make the next one better.

James graduated from medical school and moved to another state to work while Martha struggled with her studies without him. During one of her trips to visit him, Martha was involved in an accident a few miles from where he lived. She could not return to school for nine months. Martha's parents were cross, especially given that she had no business being in the city where the accident occurred. Her family nursed her back to health until she was able to return to school. Martha missed about a third of that school year and had to wait until two years to get back on track.

Martha tried to resume her relationship with James once she could leave home and return to school. It was tough trying to keep up with medical school and the demands of the relationship.

Eyes on the ball

Abraham said, "*Oh no. Never. By no means are you to take my son back there... This God will send his angel ahead of you to get a wife for my son. And if the woman won't come, you are free from this oath you've sworn to me. But under no circumstances are you to take my son back there.*"[170] Here, Abraham was expressing determination and resoluteness in the process of choosing a wife for his son. He was focused on the vision and the desired end, knowing that the new spouse would play an integral part in their lives. He had learned a few lessons about shortcuts and distractions. Even though he feared God and had a great relationship with

Sarah, he had given in to the pressure to sleep with Hagar and bear his son, Ishmael. This detour from the original plan put him in a terrible place when he had to let go of Hagar and his beloved son Ishmael to preserve the promise. It was a costly mistake, and Abraham was determined to stay with the plan in the future.

God expressed his trust in Abraham when He said: *For I have chosen him, so that he will direct his children and his household after him to keep the way of the Lord by doing what is right and just, so that the Lord will bring about for Abraham what he has promised him."*[171] Abraham, to whom much was given, was thus focused on ensuring the conditions were right for the promise to thrive, which includes the right life partner for Isaac. Parents invest so much in their children's education, growth, and development, but when it comes to the all-important aspect of marriage, they take their hands-off for fear of being seen as overbearing. The same children that previously relied on them for everything. Why did the child not ask them to take their hands off school runs, weekly extracurriculars, camps, college tuition, and more? There must be a middle ground. Parents should not choose a spouse for their children, but parents can start early to pray, discuss, share their values and lessons, and prepare their children for life and marriage, so they can stay focused and make the right choices.

To hit on the target…

Abraham was focused on fulfilling the purpose God called him to, and getting the right wife for his son, his legacy. He acted because he had *confidence in what (he) hoped for and an assurance about what (he) did not see (as yet).*[172] In all that God was doing in his life, he did not know where it was all going to end but he still chose to walk the plan and embark on a lifestyle of focus: *It was by faith that Abraham obeyed when God called him to leave home and go to another land that God would give him as his inheritance. He went without knowing where he was going. And even when he reached the land God promised him, he lived there by faith— for he was like a foreigner, living in tents. And so did Isaac and Jacob, who inherited the same promise. Abraham was confidently looking forward to a city with eternal foundations, a city designed and built by God*[173].

The author of Hebrews wrote those lines of the patriarchs in the context of their faith. Focus and faith go hand in hand. You cannot exercise your faith without focus. If you believe (have faith) that the principle of Divine activity is at work in your life, then you will be persuaded to stay focused, to stay on target. To attain success in accomplishing your vision of a successful marriage, you require a high level of focus and intentionality just like Abraham and his descendants had.

Abraham was determined to guide his family to stay focused and not run their race in vain. Abraham learned from his relationship with Lot that a partner could take you off course or stall your cause. Lot's wife did not get to Zoar, the safe place after Sodom was destroyed. Although she left Sodom, she was not focused on the goal and looked back midway – perhaps she did not believe in a better place.

Abraham and Isaac were focused, not indecisive, and would not risk falling under the category that Paul later described: *Don't you realize that in a race everyone runs, but only one person gets the prize? So run to win! All athletes are disciplined in their training. They do it to win a prize that will fade away, but we do it for an eternal prize. So I run with purpose in every step. I am not just shadowboxing. I discipline my body like an athlete, training it to do what it should. Otherwise, I fear that after (preaching to others) I myself might be disqualified.*[174]

They knew that getting married to the wrong person, though it might not appear to be a big deal now, would turn out to be

> *The principle of focus means you are disciplined and determined to walk in the other principle to ensure you win your prize.*

monumental in effect in the long run. Getting married to the 'one that catches your eye,' on that basis alone, as Samson did, could be pleasurable in the short term but become a cog in the wheel of your marriage, the bane of your life, and disqualify you from your destiny in the future. Like Isaac, you have a destiny to fulfill, and you must not allow a lack of focus to detour you.

Single and single-minded?

The principle of focus in finding and keeping the one expects that you live a life of single-mindedness, staying attentive to your purpose to ensure that you discover and fulfill God's unique plan for your life. You do not compare yourself with others or try to be like others — you stay in your lane. A life of focus is strategic, and diligent. When you are focused, you neither get into frivolous or aimless relationships nor let distractions steer you away from God's objectives for you. The signs of a bad relationship are there from the beginning, and if you are focused, you will recognize these and muster the strength to resist pressures to commit to a relationship contrary to God's best for you. You try not to have your head in the clouds but think through every choice and decision so that you do not settle for a dysfunctional relationship.

Applying the principle of focus ensures your determination to walk in the other principles to ensure you win your prize. Abraham and Isaac were focused. Their trusted servant was focused: *Trustworthy messengers refresh like snow in summer. They revive the spirit of their employer.*[175]

After he received the instructions from Abraham, Eliezer set off and was determined to return with results.

Eliezer managed the assignment with dexterity and refused to be distracted. He was fully aware of the weightiness of the task and the need to lay the foundations for building a marriage that works. He was determined to succeed. It was time for his master's heir to marry. First, he went to the right city. He did not get into the town looking for some leisure spots – a place to cool off before starting the assignment. Nor was he looking for new business deals or opportunities to expand his master's portfolio. Rather ... *he loaded ten of Abraham's camels with all kinds of expensive gifts from his master, and he traveled to distant Aram-naharaim. There he went to the town where Abraham's brother Nahor had settled. He made the camels kneel beside a well just outside the town. It was evening, and the women were coming out to draw water.*[176] Once he arrived, he began his assignment.

Abraham's camel was loaded, he was prepared. What level of preparation have you made for the marriage process? You could prepare yourself to stay focused and prepared for marriage by reading books on relevant topics, unlearning bad habits, and picking up some good new ones. You could join a community where you can learn, search for a mentor couple, embark on a personal development process and spend time praying. Your time, treasure, talent or skills, character, manners – are all part of the equipping to ensure you get the prize and the best that God has for you. Have you started praying to be led to the partner God has for you? Are you on location, and at the time that prospective ones seem to be all over the place? Are there people that seem like the one?

When you decide to be focused, you will make many adjustments. Do you know the path to where you want to go? Do you need to get off the wrong train and step onto the right one? Your friends who took advantage of your previous dysfunction will discourage you. You may have to break off from friends who do not share your values for the future. And even if your new lifestyle is lonely initially, all things will work out for your good in the end.

To be focused, you need to be alert and use your heart and head to comprehend your situations. Eliezer knelt by the well to observe: *In quietness and confidence is your strength.*[177] Sometimes, you already have a perspective formed in your minds and need to step back to hear what God is saying about a prospective individual. The servant prayed: *"O Jehovah, the God of my master," he prayed, "show kindness to my master Abraham and help me to accomplish the purpose of my journey. See, here I am, standing beside this spring, and the girls of the village are coming out to draw water. This is my request: When I ask one of them for a drink and she says, 'Yes, certainly, and I will water your camels too!'—let her be the one you have appointed as Isaac's wife. That is how I will know."*[178]

You may wonder why Eliezer would make such a request to God. Same here. That was so risky. It is like putting out a fleece which is often a dangerous way of seeking to hear God's voice. Even though it may seem narrow-minded, he was focused on his purpose. His request to God was specific, for the woman who would be for Isaac. The way everything panned out indicates a sovereign God who would work if you let Him and who will lead you into what He has already prepared for you.

> *Applying the principle of focus implies that you do not get into careless relationships.*

Focus makes identification easy

Eliezer was dedicated and focused on his assignment, so it was easy to recognize the prospective partner when she came along. Immediately he observed how Rebekah responded to his needs; he felt this was an answer to his prayers, and he progressed with his assignment. He had identified with her; he saw a kindred spirit. Identification is the basis of a relationship. He ran to meet her and made his request. When Eliezer discovered that she was from the family of Abraham's relatives, he worshipped God in appreciation. When he got to her family, he told them why he had come. *So, the man went to the house, and the camels were unloaded. Straw and fodder were brought for the camels, and water for him and his men to wash their feet. Then food was set before him, but he said, "I will not eat until I have told you what I have to say." "Then tell us," Laban said.* [179]

First, this is different from embarking on a relationship with no agenda other than to date and hang out. Eliezer had an objective in seeking the relationship.

> When sentiments are involved, we may become blind to the truth.

What I will say next may sound old-fashioned, but if you are not ready to get married in the next year or two, there is no point embarking on a relationship, just to 'date.' You can get to know someone in the context of a common or shared group. Do not seek to be the sole emotional or love interest of an individual if you are not yet ready to commit to marriage. The harsh truth is that if you are not ready and seeking to get married in the next year or two and are pushing for a relationship, you may be craving emotional or financial comfort, a place to off-load pressure or a sex partner. A relationship without defined, preferably marital outcomes, is most distracting and damaging to all parties concerned.

Eliezer defined his mission, the type of relationship Isaac was interested in, and the terms and conditions. Even when Rebekah's family wanted to observe more protocols of meeting and greeting, Eliezer refused to be distracted but stayed focused on his assignment. He needed to seal and deliver on the deal. He did not want to progress to the emotions. When sentiments are involved, we may become blind to the truth. Applying the principle of focus before you get married implies that you do not get into just any relationship. It would be best to stay focused on purpose and busy yourself with your assignment for every season of your life.

Focus breaks complications

Some people feel insecure, inferior, or incomplete unless they are in a relationship. Relationships become a crutch for them, a lean-on to feel accepted or in the league. If your friends only accept or define you by your dating or active sex life, then you may be engaging in self-harm for the benefit of others. I read somewhere that the high frequency of dating and breaking up is associated with divorce, minimizing the importance of permanence in marriage relationships.

Some people know that they are not ready to get married, say within the next five years, but they go ahead and get emotionally involved. This is often common in campus fellowships. People get engaged in a hurry just so they can 'legally' hang out saying, yes, we're engaged. The couple is together a lot – study together, eat, exchange gifts (and stolen kisses), enjoy the walks, pray together, and more. They are the envy of all; they are super entangled emotionally and may start to sleep together in some cases. When these relationships do not lead to marriage, and people decide to go their separate ways, someone is usually hurt and scarred. Many young people in ill-timed relationships become emotionally tied or connected and cannot extricate themselves until after the damage has been done. For some, pregnancy results and abortions are the order of the day because 'the good thing' happened out of time.

Soul ties from past relationships have led to many into marriages that should not have been and many carry emotional baggage in an eventual marriage. There is no point in becoming worked up over a relationship when you are not ready for marriage or intend to get married anytime soon. Unfocused and ill-timed relationships are a form of 'defrauding' the other. Paul, writing to the Thessalonians about sexual immorality, self-control, and managing passions, recognized that people could defraud or take advantage of others' weaknesses and warned that God would not take it lightly: *"It is God's will that you keep away from sexual sin as a mark of your devotion to him. Each of you should know that finding a husband or wife for yourself is to be done in a holy and honorable way, not in the passionate, lustful way of people who don't know God. No one should take advantage of or exploit other believers that way. The Lord is the one who punishes people for all these things. We've already told you and warned you about this. God didn't call us to be sexually immoral but to be holy.*[180] All the chats, late nights texts (evolving to sexting), and nude shares that whip up emotions result from a lack of focus, distract your focus, and sets you up for failure in marriage.

The single eye

Being focused before you commit implies that you choose to discipline yourself and not embark on unnecessary entanglements. Stay focused on developing yourself physically, spiritually, and emotionally rather than getting involved in a relationship when you are not ready. In addition, when connected to the principle of timing, a life of focus suggests that there is a purpose (focus) for every season (time) of your life.

For example, while in school, focus on being at your best in your studies, developing skills and character that will take you the extra mile in life. In the later learning phase of your life, create a bucket list of things you would like to accomplish in life, dream boldly — learn an instrument, a new business, skill, write a book, volunteer to go on missions, make a difference – be gainfully engaged. An idle mind, I rephrase, is a breeding ground for emotional invaders. There will be so much freedom and liberty to love waiting for you, with the right partner, at the right time.

Focus on having a single heart, a desire for God, and an undivided devotion towards Him: *And I will give them singleness of heart and put a new spirit within them. I will take away their stony, stubborn heart and give them a tender, responsive heart*[181]. Some Bible versions have called it a state of one heart, sincerity, simplicity, and gladness of heart[182]. Good practice for marriage! A focused and single heart is a place of responsiveness that helps you always be your best. When focused, your best values of integrity, obedience, truthfulness-to-self come to the fore.

> A life of focus is your gift - back to God that guarantees your well-being

Being focused or single-minded may seem challenging. However, remember that all you have within you to do life with is God's gift to you. What you eventually make of your life is your gift back to God, yourself, and humanity. One of your gifts back to God is a life of focus, and it works for you and guarantees your well-being: *I will give them singleness of heart and action, so that they will always fear me and that all will then go well for them and for their children after them.*[183] To receive God's best for marriage requires a focused life. A focused person is alert and aware of who they are lest they sleep off and the enemies sow weeds in their garden.

Jesus also speaks of focus in terms of having one vision: *The light of the body is the eye: if therefore thine eye be single, thy whole body shall be full of light. But if thine eye be evil, thy whole body shall be full of darkness.*

If therefore the light that is in thee be darkness, how great is that darkness! No man can serve two masters: for either he will hate the one and love the other; or else he will hold to the one and despise the other. Ye cannot serve God and mammon.[184] Literally, the first part speaks of the health of the eye, and the second part likens a healthy vision to a life of focus. A single, focused eye is full of light and clarity- and there is power in clarity. Further, your eye influences your vision and your ability to be guided in finding and attracting the love of your life.

In another sense, your vision is a picture of what you hope to achieve, your expected end. Without a clear vision, a purpose is destroyed: *Where there is no vision, the people perish*:[185] At the individual level, what is your vision of the kind of spouse you will be, that your spouse will be, and the kind of marriage you desire? A relationship and subsequent marriage with no vision can end in darkness, conflicts, and pain. Not having a vision or focus for your marriage and how to achieve it is like leaving your life to chance, 50 – 50, like serving two masters. While speaking of a single, focused eye, Jesus said, "*No one can serve two masters. For you will hate one and love the other; you will be devoted to one despise the other.*" Focus fosters devotion both to each other and to the success of the union, and don't all relationships need that? Your lifestyle and values will determine your choices, which determine the results in the end. "Your direction, not your desire, determines the destination and result," Andy Stanley wrote.

So, a single eye or to be single-minded signifies a sense of focus on a vision. Similarly, a double vision (di-vision) or double-mindedness is a divided focus and will not yield good results. Your eye must be single for every season of life, especially when it is time to choose a life partner. For instance, prospecting several relationships with say, three different people and asking God to show you which of them is the one will be futile.

Focus in wisdom

Staying focused on God helps you choose wisely and decisively before you advance. Eliezer showed that he had faith, he was wise and was not double-minded. When asking for or seeking a spouse, do not be double minded: *If any of you lacks wisdom, you should ask God, who gives generously to all without finding fault, and it will be given to you. But when you ask, you must believe and not doubt, because the one who doubts is like a wave of the sea, blown and tossed by the wind. That person should not expect to receive anything from the Lord. Such a person is double-minded and unstable in all they do.*[186] David prayed: *My heart is fixed, O God, my heart is fixed: I will sing and give praise*[187]. His heart was focused, steadfast, confident in God, on his path to becoming a great king and administrator. Although polygamous, a king in his time, David had some great relationships as shown in recorded conversations with his spouses. I thought it was rather serendipitous the way he met and later married Abigail.

With little or no preparation, compared to the investment in careers, possessions, and acquisitions, many marriages are not planned with the precision and focus they deserve. Do you know what it takes to enjoy the marriage you desire and deserve? Are you focused on preparing for the marriage of your dreams, or do you assume that because you are in love or that it is the right person, things will 'naturally fall into place?' As with much else that go well in life, focus on God's principles for preparing for a successful marriage. Abraham Lincoln is quoted as saying, 'I will study and prepare, and someday my opportunity will come.' He also said, '"Give me six hours to chop down a tree, and I will spend the first four sharpening the ax." This will take a deep sense of purpose, intentionality, and focus in achieving your objective – and in this case a loving and lasting relationship with the person of your dreams.

Immediately Eliezer connected with Rebekah and observed that he had likely met the prospective wife for Isaac, an answer to his prayer, he progressed with his assignment. As a result of his focus on the project, it was easy to recognize a prospective partner when she came along. Focusing on a vision for your marriage will enable you to discern fakes. You will encounter many people on the road of destiny, but a divine connection with the one for you is easier when your vision is God-given, clear, and focused. Vision, when clear, is a recruiter. The right one that identifies, connects, and is suitable and 'meet' for you will be able to run with you at your pace. Habakkuk wrote: *"Then the Lord answered me and said: "Write the vision and make it plain on tablets, that he may run who reads it.*[188]

You do not need to get involved in just any relationship to find the one, that is trial and error. Staying focused enables you to maximize your life, identify and take advantage of opportunities to connect with the love of your life when you encounter them. The principle of focus works in your relationship and all areas of your life. Living a focused life and staying on your destiny's path will guarantee more success in life. You will not be confused or double-minded.

Chapter 13
The principle of attraction

Now the young woman was very beautiful... [189]

Kunle and Kemi got married after an opportune meeting at the Glasgow airport on their way home for the Christmas holidays. Their connecting flight was delayed, so they were together at the airport longer than they planned, but they enjoyed every minute — chatting and getting to know each other. They discovered that they had a couple of mutual friends. It was undoubtedly love at first sight; they could see they were mutually attracted to each other. Kunle admired Kemi's beautiful accent. She was tall, smooth-skinned, and with an elegant frame. All through that holiday, they hung out a lot and were able to visit each other's families. Kemi was excited about meeting Kunle - he was like a Christmas gift, worth her investment in that ticket to travel home. She could not wait to see how the relationship would evolve.

Even though Kemi was from a wealthy family, she did not experience the love and attention every child should enjoy since her mum and dad separated when she was young. Both parents remarried, and she had to live with her dad and stepmom to gain an international education. Kemi hoped Kunle would take her away from her home situation speedily and meet the deepest longings of her heart. Back in the UK, she could not wait for the weekends to come, so she would travel to his city to be with some friends so she could see Kunle. Kunle was equally smitten; what were they waiting for, Kemi thought? Kemi pushed for some permanence in the relationship, and they got married as soon as they found a date over the summer that worked for both families.

From the events planning to the wedding ceremony and eventual moving in together, emotional outbursts were the order of the day. Kemi was a perfectionist and would blame Kunle for every mistake and question his motives. She checked his phones regularly to see who he had interacted with and where he had been all day or after work. She would make so much fuss about why Kunle did not call or text during the workday. She was sad whenever Kunle forgot to kiss her or commend her before leaving for work. Kemi loved Kunle but would flare up if he made any plans that did not include her. Initially, he thought it was because she was in transition, looking for a new job, having resigned to move to his county. It seemed that she expected Kunle to fill the gap of a mum and dad that she had missed growing up. Kunle was trying, but the demands were beginning to gnaw at his patience. Kunle was frequently drained emotionally. Soon, Kemi began to resent Kunle since he could not meet all her expectations.

The principle of attraction expects that you should be attracted to the person you desire to marry.

Kunle assumed he had met a confident woman at the airport that fateful day but was concerned that he had married what he later described as an emotional liability. The initial fireworks that brought them together could not be compared to the frequent wars between them. Kemi's love was as hot and passionate as her anger. Kunle and Kemi are still married, but their relationship is strained, and though they live under the same roof, Kunle lives like he is walking on coals and tries to avoid her as much as possible.

Kunle was attracted to Kemi's outward appearance and prestige but had not spent sufficient time to understand her heart's condition. When a man meets a woman, he is often first appraising her physical attributes, and if he is drawn to her, he wonders who she is on the inside and if he can have something to do with her — likewise, the womenfolk. The eyes, they say, are the first to taste the meal. While some women are not as drawn to physical attractiveness as much as to a man's personality and what he has to offer (yes, including the monetary aspects), attraction is an essential consideration for getting married to someone.

First a heart connection

The principle of attraction is coming as one of the last principles, yet it is the one that most people place first and make their priority. While the principle of attraction expects that you should be attracted to the person you desire to marry, it is not enough basis to choose an individual. Getting attracted to one's physical features is not sufficient for a commitment to last a lifetime. Attraction is more than skin deep. It is beyond physical. Nevertheless, attraction spices up relationships. When Eliezer saw Rebekah, her beauty caught his attention. Synonyms for 'beautiful' include attractive, lovely, or stunning. He must have had an eye for beauty, and knew what his master's son would appreciate, which adds, of course, to why Abraham entrusted him with the task of embarking on this quest.

Genuine attraction is first a heart connection, something beyond the physical appearance that pulls you to the other. The individual may not be as beautiful or as handsome as a model or your friend's partner, but they are simply perfect to you. You are drawn to them — there is a pull, which is best experienced when the attraction is mutual. Incidentally, what attracts you to a particular person may be what repels another from them.

Who's that girl?

Growing up, we danced to the popular song *who's that girl* and wanted to be that girl. Boaz had a *'who's that girl?'* moment when he saw Ruth for the first time. He paused to have another look: *…And as it happened, the field where she found herself belonged to Boaz, this relative of Naomi's husband. Boaz arrived from the city while she was there. After exchanging greetings with the reapers, he said to his foreman, "Hey, who's that girl over there?"*[190] Boaz had just returned to the fields to check up on his workers as they brought in the harvest. Even with numerous workers in the field, Boaz noticed and was drawn to this 'different' young woman gleaning in his field and he could not hide his surprise. There must have been several women in the area that day, but Ruth stood out to him, and Boaz inquired about her. She had caught his attention, and his servants told him that Ruth was Naomi's daughter-in-law.

Before Naomi encouraged Ruth to seek a relationship with Boaz, first and foremost, Boaz had noticed her. Without her saying a word, she got Boaz's attention and he was attracted to her and readily warned his young men not to disturb or harass her. Without a word, who you are — your aura, body language, and countenance speak to draw or repel people from you. You have a presence. You have an aroma. Paul describes the aroma or fragrance of a godly person: *Now he uses us to spread the knowledge of Christ everywhere, like a sweet perfume. Our lives are a Christ-like fragrance rising up to God. But this fragrance is perceived differently by those who are being saved and by those who are perishing. To those who are perishing, we are a dreadful smell of death and doom. But to those who are being saved, we are a life-giving perfume...*[191]

> Without saying a word, who you are- your aura, your body language and countenance are speaking, drawing, or repelling people from you.

You have a fragrance; beyond what you expect the physical perfume you wear to portray. Everyone exudes something, life, or death. You are a spirit living in a body. Your body is only a vessel covering or carrying who you are while reflecting your physical features and outward expressions. Most of the time, people see and are attracted to the dressed-up physical and outward self. However, there is a more profound person within and a deeper place and level of attraction – in the spirit. By God's sovereignty, He has endowed some with more of the best physical features and others with questionably much less: *"What sorrow awaits those who argue with their Creator. Does a clay pot argue with its maker? Does the clay dispute with the one who shapes it, saying, 'Stop, you're doing it wrong!' Does the pot exclaim, 'How clumsy can you be?' How terrible it would be if a newborn baby said to its father, 'Why was I born?' or if it said to its mother, 'Why did you make me this way?'"*[192] Don't ask, don't tell.

Before Boaz spoke to Ruth, something about her resonated with him even though neither had anticipated what it was. Attraction is a form of communication that facilitates connection. Communication is getting information across to another and hopefully getting feedback. Communication is verbal and non-verbal. Verbal communication has to do with spoken words and sound, while non-verbal is via every other way without a sound. Renowned marriage counsellor Norman Wright stated in his book, *Starting out together*, that in communication, the words we use (content) account for only 7% of our expressions. Attitude (including tone of voice) accounts for 38% of your communication, while body language, which includes elements of attraction, says more (55%) most of the time. Your intentions, personality, temperament, and character speak, connect, attract, or repel people without you saying a word.

The principle of attraction is an essential element in finding and choosing the love of your life. Attraction is better mutual and should not be forced. You may meet someone for the first time and find them physically unattractive, but when you get to know them better, they may end up becoming more appealing to you. Different qualities will endear you to people, including but not limited to their attitude, beauty, appearance, friends, lifestyle, character, knowledge, wealth, profession, family background, ethnicity, faith, and talents. What attracts you is often related to the way you are wired. Even when you find yourself physically attracted to someone, your individual backgrounds, temperaments, experiences, and mindsets influence your decisions about settling on them as the choice of a spouse. Solomon's counsel comes to bear: '*Guard your heart above all else, for it determines the course of your life.*'[193] Because '*As a man (even subconsciously) thinks in his heart, so is he*'[194].

Physical attraction makes it easy for couples to enjoy each other in their relationship. In some settings where marriages are arranged, it is acceptable that you do not necessarily have to be attracted to your prospective spouse to get married to them. Attraction grows. I have heard that in some religious settings, the leaders may also match future spouses as they deem fit, so attraction as a primary basis for the union takes a back seat. One of the biggest concerns for 'arranged' marriages is the fear of a lack of compatibility or attraction. Nevertheless, God, the ultimate matchmaker, is wise, kind, and in His mercy works to help marriages succeed. Marriage is to be enjoyed rather than endured. God wants you to be attracted to and be attractive to your spouse, to enjoy your spouse, and to take pleasure in being with them: *Let your wife be a fountain of blessing for you. Rejoice in the wife of your youth. She is a loving deer, a graceful doe. Let her breasts satisfy you always. May you always be captivated by her love.*[195]

People can also fake an attraction to you when trying to take advantage of you to benefit from your gifts. You may not have any control over what attracts people to you or their response to your attraction to them. Due to biological reasons, trauma, or past experiences, an individual's response to attraction may be subdued or overboard. It is wiser to sit back and reflect on what you find attractive in an individual at every point in time (and the consequences of that attraction) before you make a move toward seeking a permanent relationship with them.

Beyond what the eyes can see

Attraction may begin with the physical attributes, but you will need more for a commitment to last a lifetime. Besides physical features, you become connected to people in spirit; you may have used the phrase 'kindred spirit' or tribe before. It may not be easy at first to put physical attraction in the back seat but aim to focus your attention first on the hidden virtues of your relationship prospect: *So, we fix our eyes not on what is seen, but on what is unseen, since what is seen is temporary, but what is unseen is eternal.*[196] Another version put it this way: *There's far more here than meets the eye. The things we see now are here today, gone tomorrow. But the things we can't see now will last forever.*[197]

Indeed, deliberately searching for or looking toward the hidden virtue in the other person seems more like a mundane task, but that is where the principle of Divine activity comes to play: *I can do all things through Christ who strengthens me.*[198] If you let Him, God will help you and give you a discerning heart to see beyond the physical appearance.

> *Attractiveness may start with beauty or physical attributes, but you must build on something more lasting, the inner attributes.*

When God asked Samuel to anoint one of Jesse's sons as the next king of Israel, the process was akin to how people choose the love of their lives. Samuel, naturally, was moved by the first young men's physical appearance. The first son was tall and incredibly handsome: *When they arrived, Samuel took one look at Eliab and thought, "Here he is! God's anointed!" But God told Samuel, "Looks aren't everything. Don't be impressed with his looks and stature. I've already eliminated him. God judges persons differently than humans do. Men and women look at the face; God looks into the heart."*[199]

If Samuel, a prophet of repute, was swayed by looks and almost made a wrong choice in selecting Israel's next king, then everyone needs to take extra care not to let the power of attraction lead them to a bad choice for marriage. Thankfully, Samuel was sensitive and attentive to God's voice and was able to recalibrate. He took a step back and listened to God's leading, as you should if you are to make the right choice. You need God's help to manage your attractions, see the way God sees, and choose the right person for you, not just what your physical senses feel attracted to. You need to look beyond the physical and into the heart intentionally.

Why is the attraction to inner qualities more important? Make-up artistry is a billion-dollar industry. With make-up, you can modify your looks to be as attractive as your money can afford. However, the inner, hidden virtues that influence an individual and how they relate are more relevant and will not change unless consciously worked on. These qualities have the potential to make or mar your marriage. What does it take for someone to stick with you *'for better, for worse, for richer, for poorer, in sickness and in health, to love and to cherish, till death do us part,"* — it is not physical attractiveness.

True attraction increases with what you know about the other. If you spend more time with someone, there is a higher chance that you will get to know them better and discover what's attractive (or not) about them. You may start by being attracted to their physical features, but the inner beauty, which is mostly hidden, is much more critical. Peter cautioned: *Don't be concerned about the outward beauty of fancy hairstyles, expensive jewelry, or beautiful clothes. You should clothe yourselves instead with the beauty that comes from within, the unfading beauty of a gentle and quiet spirit, which is so precious to God.*[200] (*What matters is not your outer appearance—the styling of your hair, the jewelry you wear, the cut of your clothes— but your inner disposition. Cultivate inner beauty, the gentle, gracious kind that God delights in*[201]). And this applies to both the man and the woman.

Someone who is not physically attractive but honest, humble, resourceful, and calm will become more beautiful when you

> True attraction increases with what you come to know of the other

relate with them and value these qualities. Your attraction to others can be a choice and more intentional. You can choose to, and, train yourself to focus on the qualities you deem attractive: *Set your affection on things above, not on things on the earth.*[202] That sounds tough, right? Chocolate or fruit for a snack, anyone?

With time, beauty fades, but character lasts a lifetime: *Charm is deceptive, and beauty does not last; but a woman (or man) who fears the Lord will be greatly praised.*[203] A person's appearance may not say much about their character. Also, people are often conditioned to behave differently from their inborn temperaments. A person may appear quiet, act or dress pious, be reserved, but may not be kind or loving. Looks alone can be deceptive and are not the best judge.

Abraham's wife, Sarah, was so beautiful that she was forcefully taken over into the harem of the kings, and Abraham lied and said she was not his wife. Even though Sarah was old, they found her attractive; this must have been much more than her physical features. Sarah's inner beauty fueled her attractiveness and impacted the kind of relationship she had with Abraham.

Here is a description of the key to her attractiveness: ... *You should clothe yourselves instead with the beauty that comes from within, the unfading beauty of a gentle and quiet spirit, which is so precious to God. This is how the holy women of old made themselves beautiful. They put their trust in God and accepted the authority of their husbands. For instance, Sarah obeyed her husband, Abraham, and called him her master. You are her daughters when you do what is right without fear of what your husbands might do*[204]. Please look good, and call your spouse what you prefer, but do not forget that a gentle and quiet heart that is obedient to God makes an individual attractive.

> If Samuel, a prophet of repute, was swayed by physical appearance and almost made a wrong choice for the next king of Israel, you need to take extra care not to let the power of attraction lead you to a wrong choice for marriage.

And the man?

Few men in the Bible are described in terms of their attractiveness, perhaps fewer by their physical attributes. David was said to be ruddy, of goodly countenance, and good looking[205] while Absalom was described as very handsome: *Now Absalom was praised as the most handsome man in all Israel. He was flawless from head to foot.*[206] More so, Saul stood out as the tallest man in all Israel: *Now there was a Benjamite, a powerful man, whose name was Kish son of Abiel, the son of Zeror, the son of Becorath, the son of Aphiah of Benjamin. And he had a son named Saul, choice and handsome, without equal among the Israelites — a head taller than any of the people.*[207] How did they know or judge this? Was there a "Mr. Israel" or Miss Israel" contest? Someone was obviously keeping tab. God creates and endows; we acknowledge and admire. Hopefully, most people would rather have a person of substance, in every good sense of the word, rather than focus on merely their looks.

Attraction is indeed a powerful force when seeking or choosing the love of your life, but attraction is often overrated, especially when people say that "there is no chemistry" between them and a prospective individual, and so would not consider a relationship. Don't get me wrong; it is important to be attracted to and have a 'chemistry' with the individual you intend to spend your life with, after all, the spice of the marital relationship comes from the desire to be with this person above all others and the pleasure that the couple can derive from being attracted to each other sexually and in different ways.

It would almost be torture to live with someone to whom you feel no attraction or, in the worst case, someone in whom you find nothing desirable or pleasurable, especially when you are manipulated to think that you are hitching with them in a bid to do the 'will of God.' God is not mean. The hormones and emotions that fuel pleasure in humans was put there by God. Attraction fuels passion and pleasure. Yet, as individuals grow older and with the changing circumstances of life, the physical attributes that once wowed you into a relationship may start to wane. If your choice of a spouse was based solely on physical attraction, what would hold you together in those times?

You may struggle with a strong attraction and desire to be with the opposite sex at many points in your life, but you must control your emotions. Getting into relationships or cohabiting just because you are attracted to someone is not God's best plan for you. We live in a time where people want what they want, chose their standards to live by, and do not give room for God's word and manual for life. However, every path and direction you choose to take in life will have features that lead to a set of destinations or outcomes. It would be best if you considered the consequences of your choices to be sure your decisions will yield the results you would be happy with tomorrow. My prayer is that you will walk in the path of God's absolute best for your life.

Who is drawn to you?

Another point from the principle of attraction is to ask yourself, what kind of people do you presently find are attracted to you? From physics, you learn that a magnet will only attract metals with some iron to its field. Are the aura and personal energy you are exuding attracting the right or wrong people to you? Quite alright, a bright light will attract all kinds of insects, yet ask, who do you attract and vice versa? Who is attracted to you? On your own, you may want to attract only the successful, rich, beautiful, or handsome. And, if you dwell on those thoughts long enough, you will gravitate them into your space. What you think of most often, you likely attract to your life. However, overall, ask yourself, what is the root of your thoughts? Do your thoughts dwell on the inner qualities of trustworthiness, loyalty, love, peace, and industry that guarantee the marriage of your dreams?

Your heart, the object of your inner beauty, and the seat of your thoughts determine the course of your life. You take care of your heart by drawing close to God. The way you spend time taking care of yourself: your hair, your nails, your clothes so that people enjoy being around you, so also you should take care of your heart. There must be a balance between inner beauty and outer beauty. Out of the abundance of your heart, everything flows. Jesus said, '*A good man out of the good treasure of his heart brings forth good; and an evil man out of the evil treasure of his heart brings forth evil. For out of the abundance of the heart his mouth speaks.*'[208] What is the condition of your heart? What do you feed your soul? Your growth in character in your inner man is measured by the fruit of the Spirit - love, joy, peace, self-control, perseverance, patience, kindness, gentleness, longsuffering. It is never too late to assess the level of these qualities or these fruits in your life and begin to identify how you can develop each quality in your life.

In his classic, *as a man thinketh*, James Allen wrote that, "*The soul attracts that which it secretly harbors; that which it loves and also that which it fears; it reaches the height of its cherished aspirations; it falls to the level of its unchastened desires – and circumstances are the means by which the soul receives its own.*" You will be drawn to what you think about most often. Sometimes among friends or in your prayers, you are mouthing the opposite or an ideal. But when alone, what do you think about, who are you? You attract what you are, not necessarily, what you want or what you know is good for you. That is why the state of your heart is most critical.

Your eyes and ears are gates through which things get into your mind and heart. The activities you are involved in and the people you spend time with will strongly influence your life. The fruit you bear reflects what you have allowed into your heart. To ensure that you are getting the best results, you need to spend quality time in God's presence because there you will be changed from glory to glory as you are exposed to Him, and that fuels what you attract into your life: *But we all, with unveiled face, beholding as in a mirror the glory of the Lord, are being transformed into the same image from glory to glory, just as by the Spirit of the Lord.*[209] Moses' face shone because he had been in God's presence: *… the people of Israel could not bear to look at Moses' face. For his face shone with the glory of God*[210]. How wonderful it would be if the glory of God on your life attracted the right one to you.

In all, your most crucial task in the principle of attraction will be to work on yourself to become that beautiful person inside and out so that you can always be your best for the one that God has destined for you.

Chapter 14
The will of God

When your will is God's will, you will have your will
- Charles Spurgeon

Sarah had just celebrated her thirty-eighth birthday and wondered if she would ever get married. She had dated Brian for three years, but she decided not to continue once she realized he had cheated on her. Sarah met Andrew at her party. One of her friends had invited him, hoping she would be interested. Andrew and Sarah began to meet up on dates a few weeks later. Sarah said she knew yet again that Andrew was not for her, but she enjoyed his company, and life was so lonely, she wanted to go along, at least until the right person came along.

Sarah was not comfortable with some of the things Andrew asked her to do, but she did them anyway. Because Andrew lived more than twenty miles away, after each date, he would either spend the night at her apartment so he wouldn't have to rush to work or ask her to come over to his at the weekend. Sarah was convinced this wasn't right, but she kept up with his demands. She occasionally ordered alcohol because he wanted to have it when they were together. Andrew's drinking had no limit. She didn't want him to think she was traditional. It has been a year since she met Andrew, and one evening, he asked her if she would move in with him or either way to make their lives simpler. Sarah asked him why they weren't getting married before they moved in together, and his response surprised her.

Andrew didn't want to get married; his parents, now separated, were never married. Getting married would be too much trouble for him, and he wanted the freedom to move on whenever a relationship became unbearable. Sarah was on the fence about moving in; she had made several compromises already. She was thinking of moving in a month, hoping that Andrew would change his mind about getting married and so she could save some money. But she soon discovered she was not the only lady welcome in his space. Andy was a friend of all, including those who freely use his place for trysts. Andrew tried to convince her their relationship was a special one. Sarah was beginning to think that the future she desired was not possible with Andrew.

The will of God overrides all

As said earlier, marriage is one of the things you may have to do to fulfill your purpose or God's will for your life (if you are called to marry). God's will overrides any other principle as a basis for marriage. The will of God is the mind and intention of God concerning you and is primarily His word as written in the Bible. In His word, God has made provision for your salvation, direction, and success in life. You cannot decipher God's ways and thoughts except you read, study, and meditate on God's word regularly.

The will of God is His best plan, design, counsel, and desire for you on any matter. In the will of God, you are safe. The will of God is a 'place' you can choose to dwell, as come what may; if He is with you there, He will work for you there. For instance, God was leading the children of Israel out of Egypt. It was His will and plan for them to leave. Yet, they encountered the Red Sea, caught between drowning or death by Pharaoh's army. However, because they were in the will of God, the insurmountable obstacle before them turned into a miracle opportunity. God is committed to assuring your wellbeing in His will.

If God has spoken to you distinctly about a prospective partner, go for it! God is all-wise, and all-knowing and loves you. The principle of God's will is founded on the truth that because God said you can get married, you can if you choose to. The will of God is the ultimate confirmation you need before you get married. God's will mostly be in alignment with all other principles examined in this book. As noted in the principle of divine activity, God already knows you; He made you and has plans for your life. Even when things do not go as you planned, God's promise that all things will work together for the good of those that love Him stands - *I know the plans that I have for you, declares the Lord. They are plans for peace and not disaster, plans to give you a future filled with hope.*[211]

His will and plans for you are good plans, including the provision and choice of a good spouse. You can discover God's will in marriage, and the ease will depend on the level of your relationship with Him, your willingness to hear Him and walk with Him. God's will become more evident as you renew your mind to think the way God thinks: *Don't copy the behavior and customs of this world, but let God transform you into a new person by changing the way you think. Then you will learn to know God's will for you, which is good and pleasing and perfect.*[212] If your mind has not been renewed to think the way God thinks, it will be difficult for you to discern the perfect will of God, including in the choice of a spouse.

The popular pattern of thinking, the culture, or the way of doing and judging things in the world is primarily different from God's perspective. For instance, even though it seems popular to have sex before marriage to prove you are sexually compatible or "have a chemistry," God says, 'keep yourself pure until you get married, God already factored in your desires and need for chemistry from the closing principle of attraction. In His will, God makes all things beautiful in their time. In addition, even though a successful prospect is judged by what they do and how much they make now, God who knows the future says, He is your maker and provider and will teach you to profit and establish you in the land.

You can be transformed and renewed daily as you spend time in the word of God. Unlike other books, the Bible speaks for itself: *For the word of God is alive and powerful. It is sharper than the sharpest two-edged sword, cutting between soul and spirit, between joint and marrow. It exposes our innermost thoughts and desires. Nothing in all creation is hidden from God. Everything is naked and exposed before his eyes, and he is the one to whom we are accountable.*[213]

The word gives you the wisdom that is guaranteed to save your life! *From infancy you have known the Holy Scriptures. They have the power to give you wisdom so that you can be saved through faith in Christ Jesus. Every Scripture passage is inspired by God. All of them are useful for teaching, pointing out errors, correcting people, and training them for a life that has God's approval. They equip God's servants so that they are completely prepared to do good things.*[214] You can count on God's word. The word of God is perfect. It is the will of God.

The will of God is His perspective for your life

The will of God is His perspective or opinion about a matter, including your love life and marriage. God's perspective is most important for every situation or direction you will need in life. Why? If He is your Maker, Creator, Lord, God, and Master, then He owns and is in control of your life. If He is Alpha and Omega, knowing the end from the beginning, then who better to trust? If He says He is the Author and Finisher of your faith, then, to where else indeed can you run? It is such a shame that many people have disputed the existence of God or why He should control our lives. We cannot even ensure our breath of life or control what happens while we are asleep; how can we claim to be in charge of our lives? *Only the fool says in his heart, 'There is no God'*[215].

David says the evidence of God's existence can be seen by all: *The heavens are telling the glory of God; they are a marvelous display of his craftsmanship. Day and night they keep on telling about God. Without a sound or word, silent in the skies, their message reaches out to all the world. The sun lives in the heavens where God placed it and moves out across the skies as radiant as a bridegroom going to his wedding, or as joyous as an athlete looking forward to a race! The sun crosses the heavens from end to end, and nothing can hide from its heat. God's laws are perfect. They protect us, make us wise, and give us joy and light. God's laws are pure, eternal, just. They are more desirable than gold. They are sweeter than honey dripping from a honeycomb. For they warn us away from harm and give success to those who obey them*[216]. This is God's desire for you.

God has already sent you a Helper...

All that you need to live your life victoriously including finding and choosing the love of your life is available and close to you. Life becomes simpler when you connect with God and allow Him to guide you into what He already prepared for you, some of which you may have to fight for. Walking in this knowledge gives you power. Just as Eliezer was there to help Isaac find his spouse, God has already sent you a helper. In Genesis 24, the text of our case study, the name of Abraham's servant, who played such a pivotal role is not mentioned. His name is unknown, x, and at the beginning of the text, we said, 'let x be Eliezer' since he was mentioned in another place, Genesis 15:2, as Abraham's oldest servant: *And Abram said, Lord God, what wilt thou give me, seeing I go childless, and the steward of my house is this Eliezer of Damascus?*

It is also instructive that the servant's name is not mentioned throughout this all-important story. Why did the author of this text not print his name expressly given the many names mentioned in genealogies in the Bible? There are suggestions that he is a type of the Holy Spirit. And if he is indeed a type of the Holy Spirit, isn't this just like His self-effacing nature to not call attention to Himself? The benefit of cultivating a relationship with God is that you can receive and take advantage of the help freely given to you in the person of the Holy Spirit.

Jesus promised, *"Nevertheless, I tell you the truth: it is to your advantage that I go away, for if I do not go away, the Helper will not come to you. But if I go, I will send him to you," "But when he, the Spirit of truth, comes, he will guide you into all the truth. He will not speak on his own; he will speak only what he hears, and he will tell you what is yet to come."* God has sent you a Helper, your Ebenezer, and Eliezer to ease the process of finding, choosing, and keeping the love of your life. You will not struggle alone or in confusion. As you acknowledge and welcome Him, your journey will be easy and sweet.

We look forward to reading your successful love story!

Endnotes –
Scripture References

Prologue
[1] Genesis 24: 1 -67 MSG

Chapter 1
[2] John 15:4 -5 TLB
[3] 1 Samuel 17: 29 KJV
[4] Genesis 18: 14 NKJV
[5] Jeremiah 32:27 NLT
[6] Mark 10:27 NLT
[7] Proverbs 25: 2 NKJV
[8] Ephesians 5: 31-31a NLT
[9] Matthew 19: 3-8 NIV

Chapter 2
[10] Genesis 2: 18 -22 NLT
[11] Genesis 24:7 NLT
[12] Psalm 139:16 NLT
[13] 1 Peter 1:17 NKJV
[14] Jeremiah 1:5a MSG
[15] Genesis 2:18 KJV
[16] Genesis 2:23 KJV
[17] Matthew 6:25 -32 NLT
[18] Hebrews 11:6 NLT
[19] Isaiah 49:16 NIV
[20] Proverbs 18; 22 NKJV
[21] Romans 2:12-14 MSG
[22] Revelations 4:11b KJV
[23] Ephesians 2:10 NLT
[24] 1 Chronicles 4:9-10
[25] Genesis 32:24-28
[26] 2 Chronicles 16:9 TLB
[27] Isaiah 26:3 TLB
[28] Psalm 119:105 TLB
[29] Proverbs 4:18 NKJV

Chapter 3
[30] Genesis 24:7 NKJV
[31] Numbers 14:28 NLT
[32] Genesis 24: 11-12 GW
[33] Genesis 24: 26 -27 GW
[34] Genesis 24: 52 NLT
[35] Genesis 24: 42 -43 NLT
[36] Philippians 4:6 NLT
[37] Genesis 24: 62 -63 GW
[38] John 4; 24 NLT
[39] Luke 18:1 NLT
[40] Matthew 15: 21 -28 NLT
[41] Daniel 10:12-12 NLT

Chapter 4
[42] Genesis 1:28 NKJV
[43] Genesis 2: 15 NJKV
[44] Genesis 2: 18 AMPC
[45] Genesis 24: 34-36 TLB
[46] Matthew 25: 14 -15 NKJV
[47] Genesis 24:35 -36 NIV
[48] Genesis 25:5 NIV
[49] Genesis 18:18 NIV
[50] Genesis 26:12-14 NIV
[51] 1 Timothy 5:8 NLT
[52] 1 Corinthians 11:9 NLT
[53] Proverbs 18:22 NLT
[54] Genesis 24:13 -15 NLT
[55] Genesis 29:9 NLT
[56] Ecclesiastes 9:10 NLV
[57] Ruth 2:2-3 NLT
[58] Joshua 2: 8 NLT
[59] Habakkuk 2:2 TLB
[60] Ecclesiastes 3: 1-8 NLT
[61] Psalm 139:16 NLT
[62] 2 Peter 3: 8 NIV

[63] Ecclesiastes 3:11 NLT
[64] Isaiah 30: 21 NLT
[65] 1 Chronicles 12:32 NLT
[66] Genesis 24: 10- 11 NKJV
[67] Psalm 37:23 NLT
[68] Genesis 2: 24 NLT
[69] Genesis 24: 16 NLT
[70] Genesis 29: 16 -20 NLT
[71] Genesis 29: 21 -30 NLT
[72] Isaiah 28:16b NKJV
[73] Proverbs 19:2 MSG
[74] Psalm 105: 17-19 NLT
[75] Genesis 24: 20 -21 NKJV

Chapter 6

[76] Habakkuk 2: 3 TLB
[77] Psalm 68:6 NKJV
[78] Genesis 24:2-4 NLT
[79] 2 Corinthians 6:14 NKJV
[80] Deuteronomy 22:10 NLT
[81] Genesis 24:2 -4 NLT
[82] Genesis 11: 31 NLT
[83] Genesis 24: 5-7 NLT
[84] Genesis 26: 34- 35 NIV
[85] Hebrews 12:16 NIV
[86] Genesis 36:1-3 NKJV
[87] Genesis 34: 2 NKJV
[88] 2 Chronicles 8:11 NLT
[89] Warren Bennis, Finding the Love of your life
[90] 1 Kings 11: 1-5 NLT
[91] Deuteronomy 7:3-4 NLT
[92] Genesis 28: 1-2 NLT
[93] Matthew 11: 28-30 NLT
[94] Proverbs 4:23 NIV
[95] 2 Corinthians 6:14 NIV
[96] 1 Corinthians 6: 15-16 NLT
[97] Genesis 24:50 NLT
[98] Genesis 24: 57 -58 NLT
[99] Genesis 24: 3-4 ESV
[100] Genesis 24: 48 -51 NLT
[101] 2 Corinthians 5:17 NKJV
[102] Judges 14: 1-3 NLT
[103] Exodus 20:12 NLT
[104] Ephesians 6: 1-3 NLT

Chapter 8

[105] Proverbs 21:1 NLT
[106] Proverbs 18: 16 LEB
[107] Genesis 24: 21-22 NLT
[108] Proverbs 18:16 NIV
[109] Genesis 24: 29-31 NLT
[110] Genesis 24: 52-53 NLT
[111] Proverbs 17:8 NIV
[112] Deuteronomy 16:19 NLT
[113] 2 Corinthians 8:12 NIV
[114] Mark 12: 42-44 NLT
[115] Ruth 2: 8-13 NLT
[116] Ruth 2:14 NLT
[117] Ruth 2: 15-16 NLT
[118] Proverbs 18: 22 NLT
[119] Ruth 3:15 -17 NLT
[120] Genesis 32: 14-21 NLT

Chapter 9

[121] 2 Kings 5: 26b NLT
[122] Romans 8: 2 KJV
[123] 1 Peter 4:10 NLT
[124] Philippians 2: 13 ESV
[125] Genesis 24:16b -20 MSG
[126] Philippians 2:5-8 NLT
[127] Philippians 2:3 GW
[128] Galatians 6;10 ESV
[129] Proverbs 21: 5 NLT
[130] Proverbs 12: 24 ESV
[131] Ephesians 6: 6 -8 NKJV
[132] Genesis 2: 18 GW
[133] Proverbs 22: 29 KJV
[134] Matthew 20: 25 -27 NLT
[135] Exodus 23: 25 NLT
[136] Isaiah 11: 9 KJV
[137] Exodus 36:1 NLT
[138] Ecclesiastes 9: 10a NKJV
[139] Galatians 6:9 ESV

Chapter 10

[140] Philippians 2: 5 -9 NIV
[141] Galatians 6:9 ESV
[142] Psalm 23: 1-3 NLT
[143] Genesis 24: 62-63 NLT
[144] Galatians 5: 22-23 NLT
[145] Genesis 24: 62-63 NLT

[146] Proverbs 4: 18 NLT
[147] James 4:8 NLT
[148] Jeremiah 33:3 NLT
[149] Romans 8:16 NKJV
[150] Ecclesiastes 4: 11-12 NLT
[151] Psalms 16: 11b ESV
[152] Nehemiah 8: 10b NLT
[153] Ruth 1:16 NLT
[154] Ruth 2: 11-12 NLT
[155] Luke 16: 13 NKJV

Chapter 11
[156] Matthew 6: 21 NKJV
[157] Genesis 24: 16 GW
[158] Matthew 6: 22 NLT
[159] 1 Thessalonians 4: 3-4 NLT
[160] Esther 2:2 NLT
[161] 2 Timothy 2: 20 -21 NLT
[162] 1 Corinthians 6: 15 -20 NTL
[163] Genesis 34: 2-4 KJV
[164] Psalm 103:12 NLT
[165] 2 Corinthians 5: 17 NKJV
[166] 1 Thessalonians 5: 22 KJV
[167] 2 Timothy 2: 22 KJV
[168] Romans 8: 2 KJV

Chapter 12
[169] Matthew 5: 8 NLT
[170] Genesis 24:6-8 MSG
[171] Genesis 18:19 NIV
[172] Hebrews 11:1 NIV
[173] Genesis 11: 8-10 NLT
[174] 1 Corinthians 9:24-27 NLT
[175] Proverbs 25:13 NLT
[176] Genesis 24:10-11 NLT
[177] Isaiah 30:15b NLT
[178] Genesis 24:12-15 TLB
[179] Genesis 24: 32-33 NIV
[180] 1 Thessalonians 4: 3-7 GW
[181] Ezekiel 11:19 NLT
[182] Acts 4:26 NKJV
[183] Jeremiah 32:39 NIV
[184] Matthew 6:22-24 KJV
[185] Proverbs 29:18 KJV
[186] James 1:5-8 NIV

[187] Psalm 57:7 KJV
[187] Habakkuk 2: 2 NKJV

Chapter 13
[190] Ruth 2: 3-5 The Living Bible
[191] 2 Corinthians 2:14 -16 NLT
[192] Isaiah 45: 9 -10 NLT
[193] Proverbs 4:23 NLT
[194] Proverbs 23:7 Amp
[195] Proverbs 5:18 NLT
[196] 2 Corinthians 4:18 NIV
[197] 2 Corinthians 4: 18 MSG
[198] Philippians 4: 13 NKJV
[199] 1 Samuel 16:6-7 MSG
[200] 1 Peter 3: 3-4 NLT
[201] 1 Peter 3: 3-4 MSG
[202] Colossians 3:2 KJV
[203] Proverbs 31:30 NLT
[204] 1 Peter 3: 3-7 NLT
[205] 1 Samuel 16: 12 KJV
[206] 2 Samuel 14: 25 NLT
[207] 1 Samuel 9: 1-2 BSB
[208] Luke 6: 45 NKJV
[209] 2 Corinthians 3: 18 NLT

Chapter 14
[210] 2 Corinthians 3: 7b NKJV
[211] Jeremiah 29 :11 GW
[212] Romans 12:2 NLT
[213] Hebrews 4: 12 -13 NLT
[214] 2 Timothy 2: 15 -17 GW
[215] Psalm 14: 1 KJV
[216] Psalm 19:1-11 TLB

Acknowledgments

I have received much assistance since starting this book project. The initial two chapters, now in another book, were edited by Timi Yeseibo; thank you so much! My good friend, Tony Alagbile and my big sis Ud Nwachukwu read some initial chapters and provided valuable insights that I applied overall. Ayo Iyiola would copyedit the whole manuscript to improve the flow and readability. Thank you, Ayo. Thanks also to Awele and Bruce for reading through. Lisa Wolfe graciously provided useful comments and proofread the final drafts. Thank you very much, Dr. Imina Nosamiefan for providing the invaluable final touches. I am indebted! I warmly appreciate the LoveWorks team, including Amaka Okoli and so many who have kept the flag flying high. God will tremendously bless you and build you "houses" of abundance and love.

I am immensely grateful to and for my parents — my late dad, Chief Ukachi Ikemba, and my darling mum, Nneoma Florence Ikemba. The example of your over 53 years of marriage and keeping faith with purpose has stayed with me and blessed my home. I love you so much. Special appreciation goes to my beloved siblings, my family-in-love, and my extended family – you are the giant shoulders I stand on. Your immeasurable love and support mean so much. I appreciate all my good friends, spiritual children, and our ministry partners – Thank you for all you do, and God bless you more!

I am super thankful for, and to my babies — Isaac-John, Sean-David, and Joanna-Pearl — who are such a joy to love, raise, live before, and guide to destiny. This acknowledgment cannot be complete without special thanks to the love of my life, my precious husband and apostle to the body of Christ, John Enelamah, aka PJ, with whom I do life. I love you dearly! Thank you so much for who you are and all you do.

Above all, I am forever grateful to God for the grace to start and complete this assignment.